Introduction

In recent years, the Federal Reserve has made substantial changes to its framework for monetary policymaking. These changes have included a sequence of improvements in the clarity with which the Federal Open Market Committee (FOMC) has provided information on its policy objectives, starting with the introduction of the Summary of Economic Projections (SEP) and proceeding through the publication of the Committee's Statement of Longer-run Goals and Policy Strategy, which specified a numerical inflation objective for the first time. The Statement also provided information on the Committee's broader policy strategy, indicating that the Committee will take a "balanced approach" to its two objectives of maximum employment and stable prices when they are not complementary. The changes in framework have also encompassed increased communications regarding the Committee's policy intentions—that is, how it intends to use its policy tools to achieve its policy objectives. This information has been conveyed in the Committee's post-meeting statements, in the SEP, and in the Chairman's post meeting press conferences.

These changes have come about in response to two factors: improved understanding of the value of communications and transparency in helping central banks achieve their goals, and challenges for monetary policy resulting from the financial crisis and the subsequent recession. As noted by Yellen (2012), there has been a revolution in central bank communications in recent decades as it became clear that improved communications and the consequent improved public understanding of policymakers' goals and likely future actions could enhance the effectiveness of monetary policy. In part, this shift reflected the success of inflation targeting central banks in anchoring inflation expectations and improving economic outcomes.[1]

Changes along these lines were relatively gradual prior to the crisis, but by the end of 2008, with the federal funds rate at its effective lower bound, the benefits of further changes in the framework became clearer. The Committee began using nontraditional policy tools— specifically, forward guidance regarding the path of the federal funds rate and large-scale asset purchases (LSAPs)—that required increased communications about the Committee's intentions. Once the federal funds rate is at its lower bound, communications about the likely future path of short-term rates can influence longer term rates and thus, influence spending. Moreover, research suggests that it may be desirable to offset the effects of a period at the lower bound by maintaining the funds rate at a lower level than would normally be the case given economic conditions once the economy improves—that is, there are benefits to conditional commitments to lower rates (Eggertsson and Woodford (2003); Woodford (2012b)). We use a small-scale model of the U.S. economy to examine these benefits and to explore possible ways to communicate forward guidance of the kind just described. In particular, we note that the FOMC's use of economic thresholds for the possible timing of the first hike in the federal funds rate can be seen as a way of committing to keep interest rates lower for longer than would otherwise be the case under conventional policy, and thereby improve economic outcomes.

With regard to asset purchases, the effect of purchases on the economy depends on the expected quantity of purchases and the length of time that market participants expect the Committee to hold them. As a result, clear communications about the Committee's plans are necessary if the

---

[1] See Svensson (2011) for a summary of the experience of inflation targeting countries.

purchases are to have the desired effect. However, asset purchases have to be carried out over a period of time, and making commitments with regard to asset purchases is potentially more complicated than in the case of the policy interest rate because, given the limited experience with these new tools, their effects are more uncertain and their costs are similarly difficult to assess. We use a simple, static model of the considerations underlying asset purchase decisions as a way of bringing out the possible implications for policymakers of changes in assessments of the efficacy and costs of purchases as well as in the economic outlook.

The Federal Reserve has not been alone in making changes along these lines. Other major central banks have responded to these developments in similar ways. Both the Bank of England and the Bank of Japan have employed forward guidance and conducted large-scale asset purchases. The European Central Bank has engaged in long-term refinancing operations, and recently provided qualitative forward guidance on its policy rates. Thus, while our analysis focuses on the Unites States, the results have broader application and there may be important additional lessons in experiences of those other central banks.

While central banks have made significant adjustments to their policy frameworks in recent years, the challenges posed by the financial crisis raise additional issues that policymakers will need to consider going forward. For example, while most major central banks have provided relatively clear guidance regarding their policy objectives, the protracted period at the effective lower bound may suggest that the objective of low and stable inflation might usefully be changed. In particular, some observers have suggested that a higher inflation objective, either temporarily or permanently, could help ease the constraint generated by the lower bound on nominal interest rates (see, for instance, Blanchard *et al*. (2010, echoing Summers (1991)). Alternatively, some have suggested that central banks should aim to target the level of nominal GDP, which would build some history dependence into policy and potentially improve economic outcomes (Woodford (2012b)). We use our small-scale macroeconomic model to examine the possible costs and benefits of such changes. We find that both a higher inflation target and nominal GDP targeting could contribute to improved macroeconomic outcomes. However, both changes could be misunderstood or could undermine the credibility of the central bank; in such cases, macroeconomic outcomes could be significantly worse. Because of the substantial communications and credibility problems that a change in objective could raise, policymakers will need to carefully balance the potential gains against the costs and risks before taking such a step.

Finally, the crisis has raised the issue of how central bank's traditional monetary policy objectives can be integrated with their renewed interest in financial stability. The policy response to the crisis and its aftermath has demonstrated the potential complementarities between regulatory and supervisory policies (including both prudential supervision and macroprudential policies) and "standard" monetary policy (Bernanke (2013c)). We briefly discuss how the tradeoffs between different policy objectives might be made and note that, regardless of approach, there is a need for improved monitoring of financial markets and institutions to identify and address potential vulnerabilities.

I. Recent Changes in the Federal Reserve's Monetary Policy Framework

A central bank's monetary policy framework can be thought of as having four components. The first component is the central bank's policy goal or goals and the time period over which the central bank aims to achieve them. The second is the tool or set of tools that the central bank uses to foster those goals. The third is the strategy that the central bank uses when employing its tools, and the final component is the range of communications methods that the central bank uses to convey to the public information about its decisions, intentions, and commitments (if any).[2]

The changes the Federal Reserve has made since the middle of the last decade cover all four of these categories. First, the Federal Open Market Committee (FOMC) has significantly clarified its goals, ultimately providing a specific numerical interpretation of its statutory objective of price stability and significant information about its interpretation of its full employment objective. Second, with its traditional policy tool, the target level for the federal funds rate, constrained by its lower bound since late 2008, the Federal Reserve has employed nontraditional policy tools. Specifically, the FOMC has employed an augmented version of forward guidance regarding the future path of the federal funds rate as well as undertaking purchases of longer-term securities in order to put downward pressure on longer-term interest rates. Third, the Committee has made changes to its strategy for implementing policy. In particular, with the federal funds rate constrained near its effective lower bound and the effects of nontraditional policy relatively uncertain, the Committee has moved in the direction of targeting rules by providing information on its desired outcomes for employment and inflation and assurance that it will implement the accommodation needed to achieve those objectives. Finally, the Federal Reserve has greatly expanded its communications with the public. These communications enhancements include increased information provided in post-meeting statements; an explicit statement regarding the Committee's longer-run goals and policy strategy; a quarterly Summary of Economic Projections which provides information on FOMC participants' projections of the most important economic variables, their judgments regarding the risks to their projections, and their assessments of the appropriate stance of monetary policy; and finally, the introduction of quarterly postmeeting press conferences by the Chairman.

These changes to the framework reflect a number of factors. Even prior to the financial crisis, the Committee was working to improve its communications in response to results in monetary economics emphasizing that successful communications could make monetary policy more effective (Yellen (2012)). Then following the crisis, the Federal Reserve developed and implemented new tools and employed enhancements to its communication in order to provide additional monetary policy accommodation and so help to strengthen the recovery. Many of these changes developed gradually, as the Committee carefully considered their potential benefits and costs and worked to achieve consensus on particular changes.[3] Particularly with regard to communications, it is important to realize that these changes mark a continuation of earlier developments, including the introduction of post-meeting statements in 1994, the

---

[2] An example may help clarify the various components. For a strict—if straw-man—inflation-targeting central bank, the goal would be inflation at a particular numerical level at a particular horizon (perhaps 2 percent at a horizon of two years). The tool, at least in normal times, would likely be a target for a specific short-term interest rate, implemented through some standard set of market operations. The strategy for employing the tool might be a specific policy rule, such as the Taylor (1993) rule. Finally, the communications would feature prominently a regular inflation report, in which the central bank would report on inflation developments, explain any deviation from its target, and show how it planned to use its policy tool to return inflation to its target level over the required horizon.

[3] Many of the changes in communications reflected the work of the FOMC's subcommittee on communications, headed by Governor Yellen.

announcement of the "balance of risks" following FOMC meetings in 2000, and expediting the publication of FOMC minutes from 2006 onward.[4]

A. Providing greater clarity regarding policy objectives and strategy

In recent years, the Committee has taken a sequence of steps to improve public understanding of its policy objectives (Table 1). Of course, those objectives are ultimately provided by Congress in the Federal Reserve Act, which states that the Federal Reserve's mandate is "to promote effectively the goals of maximum employment, stable prices, and moderate long-term interest rates" (Federal Reserve Act, Section 2a). In general, the Committee has judged that moderate long-term interest rates would follow if the Federal Reserve achieves its objectives of maximum employment and stable prices; hence, policymakers often refer to the "dual mandate" (Mishkin (2007a)).

While the dual mandate was formally established by Congress in 1977, until recently, the Committee had not provided more specific guidance regarding its interpretation of either "maximum employment" or "stable prices." With regard to its inflation objective, Chairman Greenspan suggested that the goal should be a situation in which "the expected rate of change of the general level of prices ceases to be a factor in individual and business decision making" (Greenspan (1988)). That goal would presumably be consistent with a low positive level of inflation, but the level of inflation that might be found acceptable was left unstated. With regard to employment, the Committee was even more circumspect, with very little quantitative discussion by policymakers of the maximum employment objective (see the discussion in Yellen (2012)). In part, the focus on the inflation objective in the 1980s and 1990s presumably reflected the fact that the high and volatile inflation in the 1970s remained a fresh memory, and the Committee was focused on bolstering its credibility in order to bring inflation down over time.

However, following the financial crisis, with a risk of very low inflation or even deflation as well as employment far short of its maximum level, the benefits of clearer communication regarding the Committee's goals were manifest. Not only would such communication improve Federal Reserve accountability, it could also improve economic outcomes by helping to anchor inflation expectations, thereby helping to avoid an undesirable further decline in inflation and allowing the FOMC to take more aggressive steps to address the crisis.

A first step toward greater clarity came with the introduction of the Summary of Economic Projections (SEP) in November 2007. The SEP offers detailed information on the forecasts of all FOMC participants (the seven members of the Board of Governors and the twelve Reserve Bank presidents) under each participant's assessment of appropriate monetary policy.[5] The forecasts include four key variables reflecting the Committee's dual mandate: the growth rate of real GDP, the unemployment rate, and overall and core inflation (as measured by the price index for personal consumption expenditures). Initially, the forecasts went out three years, so the November 2007 SEP included forecasts through 2010. While the SEP does not show the individual forecasts, it does provide the range and central tendency of the forecasts, narrative

---

[4] For a summary of changes in FOMC communications from 1975 to 2002, see Lindsey (2003).
[5] Prior to the introduction of the SEP, the Federal Reserve provided more limited forecasts in the semi-annual Monetary Policy Report to the Congress. These forecasts were considerably more modest, covering only the current year and one additional year and providing only a very brief narrative supporting the forecasts.

information on the factors that participants expect to shape the outlook, the participants' assessment of the degree of uncertainty around their forecasts, and their judgment of the balance of risks to those forecasts.

An important benefit of the relatively long time horizon for the forecasts in the SEP was that, at least in normal times, they provided considerable information on the Committee's longer-term objectives for unemployment and inflation. Since three years, at least under normal circumstances, is long enough for monetary policy to have significant effects on the economy, the projections for unemployment and inflation three years ahead would presumably be close to the Committee's longer-run objectives and the projection for real GDP growth would be close to participants' estimates of the growth of potential. For example, the November 2007 SEP projections had a central tendency for both overall and core inflation of 1.6 to 1.9 percent in 2010 and a range of 1.5 to 2.0 percent, suggesting that participants saw the inflation rate most consistent with their dual mandate to be close to or somewhat below 2 percent.[6]

The SEP could also provide indirect information on the Committee's policy strategy. For example, following a shock to the economy that moved inflation and unemployment away from their longer-run levels, the projections would show how Committee participants thought it would be appropriate to trade off achievement of the two sides of the dual mandate in returning both variables to desired levels (Bernanke (2007)).[7]

These benefits of the SEP were subsequently enhanced by the addition, in 2009, of "longer-run" projections that were defined as "each participant's assessment of the rate to which each variable would be expected to converge under appropriate monetary policy and in the absence of further shocks to the economy." This additional information provided very clear evidence regarding participants' longer-run objectives, evidence that was particularly useful following the financial crisis, when employment and inflation were far from the Committee's desired levels and might be expected to take longer than three years to return to their longer-run values.[8]

The next major step in improving Committee communications regarding its objectives was the publication in January 2012 of the Committee's Statement on Longer-Run Goals and Monetary Policy Strategy.[9] This statement, for the first time, offered a single, explicit numerical value for the Committee's inflation objective, stating that, "The Committee judges that inflation at the rate of 2 percent, as measured by the annual change in the price index for personal consumption expenditures, is most consistent over the longer run with the Federal Reserve's statutory mandate." The establishment of a 2 percent longer-run goal for inflation after many years of discussion on the Committee reflected an assessment of a number of factors (Bernanke (2012b)). Most obviously, an explicit numerical inflation objective would better anchor inflation expectations and improve central bank accountability. The selected objective also needed to

---

[6] As discussed in Mishkin (2007b), this mandate-consistent level of inflation is above zero because of measurement issues and the need to take into account the effects of very low inflation on the effective functioning of the economy as a result of the zero bound on nominal interest rates and downward wage rigidity.

[7] Of course, there is bound to be some imprecision in such interpretations because the SEP provides information on the range and central tendency of the individual economic and policy projections but does not link them for each participant. As a result, it may be difficult to interpret the projections in some cases. Moreover, the projections cover all Committee participants, without differentiating the Committee members.

[8] For example, in the January 2009 SEP, the projections for overall inflation in 2011 had a central tendency of 0.9 to 1.7 percent, while the longer-run projections had a central tendency of 1.7 to 2.0 percent.

[9] The statement was reaffirmed, without material changes, in January 2013.

balance the welfare costs of inflation over time – see, e.g., Fischer (1981) – against the need for an "inflation buffer" to reduce the risks posed by the effective lower bound on nominal interest rates and possible deflation following large shocks (Reifschneider and Williams (2000)).

The Committee was less precise with regard to its longer-run employment objective. As it noted in the statement, the maximum level of employment is a function of a range of nonmonetary factors – such as demographics, education and training, technology, and labor market structure – that are difficult to quantify and can change over time. Thus, the Committee felt that it would not be appropriate to provide a fixed numerical objective for employment. Instead, the Committee noted that its policy decisions would be informed by participants' assessments of the maximum level of employment but recognized that those assessments would be uncertain and subject to change over time. Nonetheless, the Committee noted that the SEP provided information on the longer-run normal rate of unemployment, and pointed to the central tendency of those values as a way of flexibly providing information about its expectations for employment and the labor market. This flexible approach allowed the Committee to avoid risks that could arise when different indicators of labor market conditions point in different directions, smoothing through such temporary developments and giving clear guidance about the Committee's approach.

Finally, the statement provided information on the way that the Committee would employ policy in the pursuit of two macroeconomic goals. First, the Committee noted that the goals of maximum employment and stable prices are generally complementary – that is, the establishment of low and stable inflation is beneficial for the attainment of maximum employment, and deviations from maximum employment can make it difficult to attain stable prices. However, for circumstances in which the two goals are not complementary, such as following significant shocks to commodity prices, the Committee stated that it would follow "a balanced approach" to promoting them and would take account of the size of the deviations of employment and inflation from their goals and the time horizons over which they were expected to return to mandate-consistent levels, when determining the appropriate stance of policy.

In addition to the SEP and the Statement on Longer-run Goals and Policy Strategy, the Committee has used its other communications tools to improve public understanding of its goals and policy strategy. In 2005, the Committee moved up the timing of the release of meeting minutes to provide more timely information on the reasons for Committee decisions and the range of views across participants. At the time, some on the Committee thought that the more rapid production of the minutes would allow for the postmeeting statements to provide less detail (FOMC (2005)). However, since that time, and particularly since the crisis, the Committee's post-meeting statements have increased greatly in length and complexity, roughly tripling in length from an average of about 200 words in 2006 to nearly 600 words in 2013. The statement continues to provide information on economic and financial developments, but, in light of the use of forward guidance and asset purchases to provide additional accommodation, now includes considerably more discussion of the stance of policy and the conditionality of policy going forward. Additionally, in 2011, the Federal Reserve introduced post-meeting press conferences four times a year. The press conferences were intended to "further enhance the clarity and timeliness of the Federal Reserve's monetary policy communication" (Federal Reserve (2011)). Finally, in January 2012, the Committee included in the SEP individual participants' assessments of the path for the target federal funds rate that they viewed as appropriate and compatible with their individual economic projections, as well as qualitative information on the appropriate path for the Federal Reserve's balance sheet. This information can help the public to understand the approach that Committee participants see as appropriate in response to a shock to the economy. All of these changes, as well as more standard communications tools, such as speeches and testimonies, have allowed the Federal Reserve to provide additional detail and nuance regarding its policy intentions and to convey more clearly the range of views across the Committee.

Some foreign central banks have also taken steps to improve communications regarding their objectives and policy strategy, responding to the same factors that led to changes by the Federal Reserve. The experience at the Bank of Japan (BoJ) has been most similar to that of the Federal Reserve, with the Policy Board providing increasing clarity on its goals and intentions over time. Like the Federal Reserve, the BoJ's statutory mandate does not provide a numerical inflation objective, but rather calls for the BoJ to aim policy at "achieving price stability, thereby contributing to the sound development of the national economy" (Bank of Japan Act, Article 2). In the face of ongoing deflation, the Bank indicated in 2006 that it intended to "realize price stability over the medium to long term" and that the Policy Board members understood price stability to be a year-on-year change in the consumer price index (CPI) of between zero and two percent (Bank of Japan (2006)). In 2012, the Policy Board introduced a "price stability goal in the medium to long term" of a positive range of 2 percent or lower in the year-on-year change in the CPI, and further noted that within this range it set a goal of "1 percent for the time being" (Bank of Japan (2012)). More recently, the Policy Board has set a "price stability target" of 2 percent by the same measure (Bank of Japan (2013a)). At the same time, the Policy Board provided information on its policy strategy, indicating that monetary policy would be aimed at sustainable growth and price stability "over the next two years or so" and also at longer term risks, particularly financial imbalances. This strategy was further elaborated in April, with the introduction of "Quantitative and Qualitative Monetary Easing," under which the Policy Board announced steps to achieve its price stability target at the earliest possible time, "with a time horizon of about two years" (Bank of Japan (2013b)).

In the United Kingdom, there has also been an increase in clarity regarding the objectives and approach of the Bank of England. After about a decade of development following the forced exit from the ERM in 1992, the remit of the Monetary Policy Committee in 2003 was an underlying inflation rate (measured by the 12-month change in the Consumer Prices Index) of 2 percent. Subject to that, the Bank's remit was to support the economic policy of the government, including its objectives for growth and employment (HM Treasury (2003)). However, earlier this year, with inflation running above the 2 percent target in part because of increases in administered and regulated prices as well as changes in exchange rates, both the Monetary Policy Committee and the U.K. Treasury indicated that they saw it as appropriate to "look through" even fairly protracted periods of above-target inflation rather than "risk derailing the recovery by attempting to return inflation to target sooner" (HM Treasury (2013); Bank of England (2013)). More broadly, the U.K. Government's March 2013 remit to the Monetary Policy Committee spelled out in greater detail the approach to be taken to monetary policy decisions in the context of a primary objective of medium-term price stability. In particular, the Treasury called for "an appropriately balanced approach" to the Committee's objectives, including to the tradeoffs between the inflation objective and the Committee's goals with regard to the variability of output and financial stability, as well as for greater transparency regarding the Monetary Policy Committee's decisions with regard to such tradeoffs (HM Treasury (2013)). Thus, despite what might sound like a lexicographic mandate, the Bank of England is effectively a "flexible inflation targeter."

The European Central Bank has not provided as much additional information on its objectives or policy approach in recent years. The ECB's objective for monetary policy is set by treaty to be price stability, and, "without prejudice to that objective, support of the general economic policies of the European Union" (ECB (2011)). In 1998, the ECB defined price stability to be a year-on-year increase in the Harmonized Index of Consumer Prices for the euro area of below 2 percent over the medium term. This broad definition was subsequently clarified in 2003, when the Governing Council of the ECB indicated that it would aim to keep euro area inflation "below, but close to" 2 percent over the medium term. The treaties of the European Union provide no additional guidance on how the ECB might, for example, balance the time period over which it aims to achieve its price stability objective against other objectives such as growth or financial stability. That said, the ECB's objectives have allowed the Governing Council to state that policy rates will remain at current or lower levels for "an extended period of time" given the "subdued outlook for inflation…, the broad-based weakness in the economy and subdued monetary dynamics" (ECB (2013a)).

B. Incorporating new tools and providing information on how they will be employed

The second set of changes to the Federal Reserve's monetary policy framework was the introduction of nontraditional policy tools and the consequent increase in communications regarding their use. Late in 2008, with the federal funds rate at its effective lower bound, the Committee introduced two nontraditional policy tools – forward guidance regarding the federal funds rate and LSAPs. As noted earlier, both of these tools require communication about the Committee's possible future actions. The form of this communication has changed over time as the Committee has gained experience with these tools.

B.1. Forward guidance

Over time, the Committee's communication of its forward guidance regarding the federal funds rate has changed. At the outset, the Committee indicated its expectation that economic conditions were "likely to warrant exceptionally low levels of the federal funds rate for an extended period" (FOMC (2009)). Subsequently, in August 2011, the Committee provided a specific date, through at least which it anticipated that a very low funds rate would be appropriate (FOMC (2011a)). However, the Committee was concerned that such *date-based forward guidance*, even if explicitly conditional on economic outcomes, could be misunderstood by the public, and thus in December 2012, the Committee changed its language to make the maintenance of a very low federal funds rate explicitly conditional on economic conditions—that is, *state-dependent forward guidance*. Specifically, it indicated that the "exceptionally low range for the federal funds rate will be appropriate at least as long as the unemployment rate remains above 6½ percent, inflation between one and two years ahead is projected to be no more than a half percentage point above the Committee's 2 percent longer-run goal, and longer-term inflation expectations continue to be well anchored" (FOMC (2012)).

In this section we use a small-scale model of the U.S. economy to explore the possible benefits of this sort of threshold-based forward guidance.[10] We start with background on the performance of simple instrument rules in our model, with a focus on performance in the current situation, with elevated unemployment, below-target inflation, and the funds rate at its effective lower bound. We then proceed to consideration of outcomes under optimal policy in the model, and then show that augmenting simple rules with thresholds can yield outcomes that are closer to those under the optimal rules than those that can be achieved using the simple rules.

Instrument versus targeting rules

Simple instrument rules could be part of a broad-based communications effort, providing a link between the economic outlook and likely path of the policy rate, and making policy more predictable and more effective.[11] In particular, before the recent financial crisis, simple policy rules attracted broad interest because they can provide a clear and easy-to understand benchmark for adjustments to the short-term interest rate. The value of such rules as benchmarks to help inform policy decisions comes partly from their simplicity. For example, the Taylor rule and other rules of that general form imply that the federal funds rate responds to only a small number of variables (the output gap and realized inflation in the case of the Taylor rule), with the versions differing primarily in their responsiveness to slack.[12] This simplicity makes it easy to understand how the rule prescriptions respond to changes in economic conditions.

To achieve the FOMC's 2 percent inflation objective on average, a policy rule must satisfy the Taylor principle. The remaining aspects of the design and calibration of the policy rule mainly determine the variability of inflation, resource utilization, and interest rates that will be implied by the rule. Given the extent of uncertainty and disagreement regarding the true structure of the economy, the robustness of the performance of policy rules across different macroeconomic models is a critically important characteristic and the subject of considerable research. The literature on this and other topics related to simple policy rules—which was recently reviewed by Taylor and Williams (2011)—has identified several features that govern how rules perform across a range of conventional models. A general result from the literature is that a complicated rule that is optimized to perform best in a particular model may perform very poorly when evaluated in other conventional models. The literature has, however, identified a variety of simple policy rules that are robust in the sense that they perform well across a range of models.

Accordingly, academics and policymakers have frequently looked to the prescriptions of simple rules as useful benchmarks for setting the federal funds rate.[13] Thus, the available theory and evidence on simple rules deal most fully with the implications of such rules when the policy rate is far from the effective lower bound. Unfortunately, as we discuss below, several important considerations suggest that simple rules that are quite successful in normal times may be less reliable under conditions such as those that the US economy is facing nowadays.

---

[10] See Svensson (2013) for a recent discussion of forward guidance as a monetary policy tool with an application to the Swedish recent experience.

[11] For a discussion, see the collected papers in the Taylor (1999) volume.

[12] This applies to prescriptions from a variety of monetary policy rules, including Taylor's original 1993 rule and a later version he examined in Taylor (1999a).

[13] See, for example, Meyer (2000) and more recently Kohn (2007).

While simple policy rules have many virtues, they are obviously no panacea, and it would be useful to have a framework for evaluating when rigidly following a rule is inappropriate. The approach called forecast-based targeting deserves consideration as a complement to simple policy rules.[14] In general terms, to perform policy evaluation under this approach, one examines the forecasts of goal variables under various alternative policy rules, and chooses the policy delivering the forecasts that "look best" under the policy objectives (e.g., Svensson (2003)). What gives the idea substance is the fact that optimal policy generally has implications for how the forecasted paths of goal variables should evolve—and some of these properties hold robustly across a range of models. For example, if policymaker preferences are symmetric, so that inflation and unemployment above or below objective are equally costly, then it will tend to be best to provide additional accommodation such that the medium-term projections of inflation and employment come to lie on opposite sides of their long run objectives—i.e., when projected employment is below its objective (so that projected unemployment is elevated), then projected inflation should at some point be (temporarily) above target (see, for example, Woodford (2011)). This emphasis on seeking policy settings that bring both inflation and resource utilization back toward their objectives in the medium term is the hallmark of the flexible inflation targeting approach.[15]

One might complement rule-based prescriptions with analysis of whether the implied forecasts of unemployment and inflation satisfied conditions of this variety. In this way, key principles of optimality could be brought to bear as complements to policy benchmarks implied by simple rules. However, recent developments—including decisions to cut the funds rate to its effective lower bound and to use nontraditional policy tools—may have complicated the interpretation of simple rule prescriptions. With the federal funds rate target at its lower bound, additional stimulus cannot be provided by reducing the target for the funds rate—the usual focus of simple rule prescriptions. As noted above, partly as a result, the FOMC now provides considerable forward guidance about the likely future path of the funds rate. While simple rules can help inform such forward guidance, they can do so only if combined with information on the outlook well into the future—something about which there is considerably more uncertainty than the economy's current position. A further complication is that the Federal Reserve has supplemented its traditional funds rate instrument with LSAPs, the effects of which also need to be taken into account.

We lay out here some arguments for why the special features of an economy that has spent an extended period at the effective lower bound may justify deviating from the prescriptions of simple rules—even rules viewed as dependable in normal times. When policy is constrained at the effective lower bound, however, outcomes under these rules may be very far from optimal. As recently summarized in the literature, monetary policymakers can potentially stimulate the economy and thereby mitigate the impact of the effective bound constraint by making

---

[14] Bernanke (2004) refers to this approach as "forecast-based targeting;" Svensson (2003, 2005) instead uses the term "targeting rules." For a critical comparison with instrument rules, see McCallum and Nelson (2005).

[15] To be sure, the particular confluence of shocks that results in employment and inflation differing from their desired levels, together with the specific features of the model, could result in a period in which employment and inflation are on the same side of their targets, but so long as those shocks do not change the targets themselves, in New Keynesian models under rational expectations it will be optimal for one of the two variables to overshoot the longer run objective and approach from the other side. See, for example, Svensson (2011) for a discussion of this approach in detail.

commitments about the future course of policy. An obvious question that arises is what framework should be adopted in which to make such commitments. One useful perspective, adopted in our simulations discussed below, applies optimal control theory to derive an "optimal" policy path. This path is obtained by minimizing a specific loss function (e.g., one that depends on the output gap, inflation gap, and perhaps other factors) subject to a particular behavioral model of the economy assuming that the monetary policy rule is both well understood by the public and is fully credible. A significant difficulty with "optimal" rules derived in this framework is that such rules tend to be very complex and their performance may be quite sensitive to specific features of the modeling environment. Nevertheless, a considerable body of research suggests that four robust features characterize optimal rules that are derived in the presence of an explicit effective-lower-bound constraint.[16]

a) *Exploiting intertemporal tradeoffs.* The first element of an optimal rule is that it promises that *future* policy will be more expansionary than usual after the economy no longer faces a binding effective lower bound constraint. Policymakers communicate this promise by indicating to markets that they expect to push output above potential for an *extended period* after the economy no longer faces a binding lower bound constraint. This policy takes full account of dynamic tradeoffs, including the possibility of influencing current expectations about future short rates and inflation through making promises about future policy.

b) *History dependence.* A second element of the optimal policy is that it is "history dependent," so that the extent and duration of policy stimulus in the period after the policy rises from its lower bound depends on the evolution of output and prices during the period in which policy was constrained. Intuitively, as an economy facing an effective lower bound constraint becomes mired in a deeper recession, an optimal policy would promise even more stimulus in the future in order to reduce long-term real interest rates.[17]

c) *State dependence during the tightening phase.* A third element of the optimal policy is that the timing and size of adjustment in policy rates after they rise above the lower bound depends crucially on the evolution of economic conditions. Thus, if the recovery turns out to be unexpectedly robust, policy rates could be adjusted upward relatively quickly and by a substantial amount, though to a degree that still leaves an expansionary tilt to policy.

d) *Credibility and time inconsistency.* Finally, the role of expectations in such optimal policies implies that such a strategy relies on credible communication that allows the public to understand the policy strategy. In other words, because the benefits of the optimal policy are front-loaded—i.e., reduce longer-term real interest rates—while the costs are paid later— overshooting of the inflation and output objectives—policymakers may have a strong incentive to renege on their commitments (i.e., the policy can be time inconsistent). Thus, the credibility of the central bank's commitment is a critical question because the efficacy of strategies that rely on commitment hinge on whether the private sector believes that the central bank will carry through on its promises.

Performance of simple rules in the current environment

---

[16] Eggertsson and Woodford (2003) and Woodford (2011, 2012b) provide excellent discussions of the optimal policy under commitment in the presence of a zero bound constraint.

[17] Nevertheless, at the other extreme, history-dependent strategies have been shown to perform very poorly in models in which expectations regarding interest rates or inflation are purely backward looking, such as in the widely analyzed simple model of Rudebusch and Svensson (1999).

An extensive literature has evaluated the performance of simple instrument rules when shocks are of the mild sort experienced during the 20 years before the financial crisis—that is during the so-called Great Moderation—with the result that the prescribed policy rate is almost always far enough from its effective lower bound that the bound can be largely ignored.[18] In contrast, in this section we consider the prescriptions and economic implications of simple rules in today's highly unusual conditions—a situation in which the lessons gained from analyzing rules under "normal" conditions may no longer apply. Toward this end, we carry out simulations of a small, structural New Keynesian (NK) business cycle model, subject to certain baseline economic conditions, and with monetary policy assumed to follow one of a selection of simple monetary policy rules. Each of the model, the baseline, and the rule can matter for the outcomes shown, so we briefly discuss each here, with details left to the appendix. The model is a small-scale representation of the Board staff's FRB/US model.[19] The model features three structural decision rules, one each for output, inflation and the federal funds rate, and a small assortment of equations delineating the target paths of output and inflation toward which the decision rules map out the adjustment. In broad terms, taking into account the model's representation price and wage decisions as forward-looking and its treatment of consumption and investment spending decisions as closely related to longer-term interest rates, FRB/US can be thought of as a hybrid NK model in the sense of Woodford (2003) or Galí (2008).[20] The baseline is constructed to be broadly representative of the conditions that the Federal Open Market Committee sees, as reported in the most recent Summary of Economic Projections. It features a sizable (negative) output gap that closes only slowly over time, core PCE inflation that has been somewhat below target for some time and is not expected to return to target for some time to come and (conventional) monetary policy that is presently constrained by the effective lower bound. Changing the details of the baseline outlook will change the fine points of the results but most baseline outlooks that embody the features just described will render qualitatively similar outcomes.

In what follows, we employ some or all of five policy rules, chosen to cover the main alternatives discussed in the literature. Included in our set is the canonical Taylor (1993) rule, and two variations on it. The Taylor (1999) rule is identical to the original Taylor (1993) rule except that the former puts a higher weight (of unity) on the output gap rather than 0.5 as in the original Taylor rule. These two rules are non-inertial or "static" rules—that is, the lagged values of the nominal interest rate do not enter into the rule. The inertial Taylor rule takes the 1999 specification and adds a moderate degree of interest rate inertia by setting the coefficient on the lagged nominal interest rate to 0.85.[21] Our fourth rule is the first-difference rule, which does not

---

[18] See the excellent review of this literature contained in Taylor and Williams (2011).

[19] Indeed, "small FRB/US model" was estimated by matching the impulse response properties of the rational expectations version of its larger sibling. See the Appendix and Brayton (2013) for details.

[20] The model embeds a mixture of forward and backward looking elements influencing firm and households decisions, including price and wage setting. The appendix summarizes the main features of the model including the characteristics of each of the simple rules used in the simulations.

[21] The inertia might suggest that either policy makers prefer to avoid large changes and reversals in the policy rate, or as something of a hedge against uncertainty and the policy errors that a less gradualist policy response might uncover. Alternatively, inertial rules might arise if the Committee were actually setting policy in a non-inertial manner but responding to some persistent variable that was omitted from the rule. Rudebusch (2006) presents arguments and evidence against true inertia as the primary explanation. English, Nelson, and Sack (2003) argue that both inertia and other causes seem to be at work. Yet, Woodford (2003) emphasizes that inertia would be consistent

depend on the *level* of the output gap or the *level* of the long-run quarterly real interest rate, but instead responds to the *change* in the amount of slack and the inflation rate. The absence of level conditions in rules like the first-difference has been touted as an attractive feature for reasons of robustness (see, e.g., Orphanides (2003)). Finally, although the analysis is deferred to later in the paper, we also use a nominal-income (level) targeting rule that has policy respond to discrepancies between the (log) level of nominal income and a predetermined path for that variable, subject to some partial adjustment in the federal funds rate. Each of these rules is also subject to the effective lower bound on nominal interest rates. In a later subsection, we consider augmenting these simple rules with thresholds for raising the federal funds rate.

Except where otherwise indicated, it is assumed in our simulations that private agents fully understand the future economic implications of each rule and that the central bank enjoys complete credibility. Figure 1 shows the policy prescriptions and economic outcomes for our first four policy rules. As can be seen, the first date of policy firming ranges from the onset of the simulation, in 2013:Q3, in the case of the Taylor (1993) rule, to 2014:Q3, in the case of the Taylor (1999) rules and inertial Taylor rule. All else equal, a rule that calls for keeping the federal funds rate relatively low for a longer time yields a faster decline in the unemployment rate and an inflation rate closer to the Committee's 2-percent objective. Rules that incorporate greater history dependence in the form of interest-rate smoothing, or rules that respond strongly to the level of resource utilization, as opposed to output growth as does the first-difference rule, tend to involve a longer period over which the federal funds rate is kept at its lower bound. However, the post-tightening behavior of the policy rule also has a material effect on economic outcomes. This is amply illustrated by comparing the Taylor (1999) and inertial Taylor rules which differ only in the lagged endogenous variable of the latter. As we already noted, the two rules prescribe departure from the effective lower bound at the same date, and produce broadly similar paths for the federal funds rate, at least for a time, but imply notably different paths for inflation and real activity.

Because private, rational agents are taken as having a full understanding of the rule and have complete confidence in the policymaker, they anticipate the persistence in funds rate setting beyond the period shown that is promised by the inertial Taylor rule, inflation under that rule is higher and thus real rates are lower, thereby driving down the unemployment rate faster, than under the Taylor (1999) rule. By the same token, the first-difference rule produces a more-rapid decline in unemployment than other rules in spite of an early lift-off date, an outcome that owes to the higher inflation that rule engenders. The first-difference rule does, however, produce notably more secondary cycling in the years beyond the period shown than do other policy rules. That said, the fact that current policy prescriptions vary considerably across rules illustrates a more general phenomenon: If the Committee strictly adhered to the prescriptions of these or most other simple rules, the projected timing and pace of policy firming would likely be quite sensitive to modest differences in views about the outlook, to modest changes over time in projections of real activity and inflation, and to the details of the rule.

To get a sense of the probability distribution of the date of first firming under different policy rules, we performed a set of stochastic simulations of the model, with policy governed by the

---

with optimal policy in many models. Evidence suggests the each story plays some role, but we do not take a strong position on the source of this historical phenomenon.

same four policy rules we used in the construction of Figure 1.[22,23] The four panels in Figure 2 show the distribution of dates of first increase in the federal funds rate as implied by stochastic simulations of the model assuming that the policymaker strictly follows the rule. The results suggest two general conclusions: first, most policy rules attach considerable likelihood to an early departure from the effective lower bound.[24] We will have something to say about the advisability of early departure a bit later. Second, the first point notwithstanding, there is considerable uncertainty both across policy rules and within the context of a single rule, on the likely date of departure from the effective lower bound. As can be seen, regardless of the rule, the distribution indicates considerable odds that conditions could evolve in a manner that would either call for raising the federal funds rate well into 2014 or later. This uncertainty presents some obvious challenges for forward guidance in monetary policy, particularly when that forward guidance is articulated in terms of predictions of particular dates for policy firming— that is, *date-based forward guidance*. Shifting views of the economic outlook, changes in perception of the monetary policy transmission mechanism, or merely the ebb and flow of policy Committee internal dynamics, could alter the predicted date of firming in ways that could be difficult to communicate to the public and might undermine the credibility of the central bank.

Of course, these estimated probabilities are sensitive to the specific rule used to set monetary policy in the stochastic simulations. For example, as we will discuss below, the simulated distribution shifts considerably when forward guidance is introduced via a threshold-based strategy overlaid on a given policy rule.

Our stochastic analysis showed a considerable likelihood of an early prescribed departure from the effective lower bound. However, whether such an early departure is advisable is an open question. One way of assessing this question is to consider the distributions of economic performance conditional on an early departure from the effective lower bound. We will consider this metric a bit later when we examine threshold-based strategies because such strategies provide a natural basis for comparison. Another criterion for judgment, closer to the theme of the communications challenges surrounding forward guidance, is the probability, once departure

---

[22] The stochastic simulations use 5000 bootstrapped draws from the model's historical shocks drawn over a period from 1984:Q1 to 2012:Q4, subject to the same baseline as described in the text. The model is subjected to shocks for the period from 2013:Q3 to 2018:Q4, and simulated, under rational expectations, once for each of the 22 shocked dates to complete a draw. We assume that policy is implemented beginning in 2013:Q3, subject to the zero lower bound.

[23] Using a longer date range for the stochastic shocks in our stochastic simulations, which amounts to including some larger, pre-Great-Moderation shocks, tends to shift the modal date of departure from the effective lower bound to the left. The logic for this result is akin to option pricing theory. The policy rule under the effective lower bound can be thought of as an option to leave the lower bound but not the obligation to do so. The value of that option, and the probability of leaving the lower bound are a positive function of the variance of shocks. Thus the inclusion of larger shocks manifests itself in more probability mass at earlier firming dates.

[24] It is interesting and noteworthy that the rule that calls for the earliest departure under baseline conditions, the Taylor (1993) rule, is the one that has the smallest mass for departure for early dates. This is a manifestation of the rule's low sensitivity to economic conditions which means that it takes a less likely configuration of net positive real shocks to reduce the shadow price on the effective bound constraint to zero than is the case for, say, the Taylor (1999) rule. In contrast, the first-difference rule predicts a high incidence of early departure from—and of return to—the effective lower bound. This is because the first-difference rules responds to changes in economic conditions, but eschews levels, meaning that a short string of positive surprises can call for policy tightening which might be appropriate when the initial output gap is close to zero but will often be inappropriate when the gap is substantially negative.

has occurred, that the policy rule will prescribe a return to the effective lower bound within a particular interval of time. Clearly forward guidance that centers on departure dates from the effective lower bound will be less reliable and less effective if that departure turns out to be a temporary occurrence. Figure 3 shows the probability of return to the effective lower bound conditional on the date of departure, marked on the x-axis, for the four policy rules. Three key points can be gleaned from the figure. First, depending on the policy rule, there is a substantial probability that forward guidance on the departure date, even if is initially accurate, will eventually be met with "regret" in the sense that a return to the effective lower bound is likely. Second, the probability of return to the effective lower bound varies widely across policy rules, with high likelihood for the "static" policy rules—the Taylor (1993) and (1999) rules—and much lower probabilities for the inertial Taylor rule. Third, for some rules, most notably the first-difference rule, but also to a lesser extent for some other rules, the likelihood of regret in this sense of the term declines as the date of the first federal funds rate increase is deferred by economic circumstances.[25]

Simple rules and optimal policy in the current environment

As discussed above, given the effective lower bound, policymakers face constraints when considering strategies to provide additional stimulus. "Optimal" policy simulations of macroeconomic models can provide some insight into strategies that may be desirable. Figure 4 shows the implications of two strategies, an "optimal policy" under commitment and one under discretion, and compares these to one of our simple rules, the inertial Taylor rule. To compute the optimal policy, we assume that policymakers place equal weight on penalizing squared deviations of PCE inflation from its target of 2 percent, on keeping the unemployment rate close to the natural rate of unemployment, which is taken currently to be 5½ percent, albeit declining gradually over time to eventually reach 5¼ percent, and on minimizing changes in the federal funds rate.[26] Under *commitment*, the Committee is willing and able to credibly commit (conditional on economic outcomes) to future policies that are generally more expansionary than usual in order to stimulate activity today, despite the temptation to tighten policy early that arises in such cases. In the *discretion* case, the Committee still sets an optimal policy, but on a period-by-period basis.

Under the commitment strategy, optimal policy, shown by the purple dot-dashed line, the nominal federal funds rate is held near its lower bound well into a period of economic expansion. Of course, this commitment implies that the unemployment rate eventually falls below its natural rate for a time and inflation rises slightly above its long-run objective value. It is the promise to remain accommodative and not prevent future above-target inflation and below-target unemployment that lowers current long-term interest rates and thereby stimulates activity today.

---

[25] Care needs to be taken in assessing the probability of return to the effective lower bound for departure dates that are late in the period shown as the number of departures covered under these circumstances can be small, as indicated by the bars in Figure 2.

[26] Per period losses are discounted with a quarterly discount factor of 0.99. As noted in footnote 20, the presence of a penalty on the change in the federal funds rate can be justified on the grounds of a desire for robustness or simply as a preference of policy makers. In stochastic simulations of the FRB/US model, the weight on this factor in the loss function produces variability in the funds rate that approximates the historical record, once one corrects for the low-frequency historical drift and volatility of inflation.

In contrast, the discretionary policy, which does not constrain future actions, prescribes a considerably more rapid pace of tightening as the economy recovers, as shown by the red dashed line; this trajectory ensures that inflation does not rise above the 2 percent target rate and that unemployment does not fall appreciably below its natural rate, but also results in substantially poorer economic performance, on average, over the next decade.

Both of these policies involve later departures from the effective lower bound than do simple rules, including the inertial Taylor rule shown in the figure by the black solid line as a reference. Outcomes under this simple rule are substantially worse than those under the optimal policies.[27] There are two important differences between the inertial Taylor rule and optimal policy. First, the inertial Taylor rule is somewhat less responsive to resource utilization, which appears to account for the difference between this rule and the discretion strategy. Thus, the inertial Taylor rule strategy involves raising the federal funds rate earlier, and keeping it above the path implied under discretion after the firming date. Second, the commitment strategy involves managing expectations regarding future policy actions and remaining accommodative for a substantially longer period: These conditional commitments lead to much better performance, on average, with only moderate overshooting of inflation of the 2-percent target rate and undershooting of unemployment in relation to the natural rate.[28]

We now turn to an evaluation of how each policy rule operates under an alternative scenario. Such an analysis is critical to gauging the robustness of the relative performance of the various rules under a range of conditions, and not just under the baseline outlook (particularly as the economy may evolve in quite unexpected ways). In this scenario, a sequence of adverse demand shocks lead to a larger absolute output gap than in the baseline; in the second scenario, adverse price shocks boost core PCE inflation significantly. As can be seen from Figure 5, the adverse demand shock widens the initial output gap from about -3 to -5 percent. The different strategies lead to more distinct differences in outcomes: The inertial Taylor rule provides the most accommodation because of its strong response to resource utilization as well as the policy inertia that introduces a form of history dependence, whereas the Taylor (1993) strategy provides the least accommodation and shows a performance that is especially poor. In all cases, the simple rules do not perform nearly as well as the optimal policy under commitment in the presence of a negative demand shock: Optimal policy elicits a sharper decline, and a more noteworthy overshooting, in the unemployment rate, relative to the natural rate, than does the inertial Taylor rule. The optimal policy strategy commits to remaining accommodative for a long period, which involves promising that later in the decade inflation will overshoot its goal value by a larger margin, which in turn implies lower long-term real rates early in the scenario, supporting a more rapid improvement in real activity. It is interesting to note that the real federal funds rate is higher at longer horizons (i.e. beyond 2019) under optimal policy than under the simple rules, which keeps the output gap slightly negative for a time, inducing inflation to eventually fall

---

[27] Measured by the same loss function used to construct the optimal policies, the rankings of policy rules under the baseline scenario, over the period from 2013:Q3 to 2018:Q4, from best to worse are as follows: commitment > discretion > first-difference rule > inertial Taylor rule > Taylor (1999) > Taylor (1993).

[28] The logic also underlies the strategy proposed by Reifschneider and Williams (2000). These authors argued that in the aftermath of a prolonged period when the short-term nominal interest rate has been constrained by the zero bound, the short-term nominal interest rates should be held lower for longer than would be suggested by the conventional rule. That is, as a recovery from an effective lower bound episode proceeds, monetary policy keeps the funds rate lower than a rule would ordinarily call for in order to make up for past shortfalls in conventional monetary policy.

significantly toward its 2-percent target. In short, the longer-horizon commitment to tighten policy improves the near-term trade-off between unemployment and inflation compared with results using the simple rules. In the light of the high initial level of unemployment, this improved trade-off induces policymakers to pursue a highly-accommodative policy in the near term: Inflation temporarily rises above 2 percent under the optimal policy – noticeably higher than under the simple rules – but this cost is optimal because it allows a further increase in unemployment to be avoided. Although the policies considered here were not designed specifically for this purpose, these results are reminiscent of the literature on risk-sensitive policy design that points to another reason to keep the policy rate at the effective lower bound for longer than would otherwise be appropriate. In effect, a strategy of remaining lower for longer provides precautionary stimulus when symmetric shocks confer asymmetric losses as they do at the effective lower bound.[29]

Using forward guidance for the federal funds Rate to implement targeting rules

A potential difficulty with commitment-based strategies is that their effectiveness depends on influencing the public's beliefs about the policy as many as five years or more ahead. Moreover, as we noted above, the optimal commitment strategy involves adhering to low settings of the federal funds rate well after the point at which the unemployment rate has returned to a level consistent with full employment. Thus, the benefits of these strategies are frontloaded while the costs are incurred later, providing an incentive to renege—that is, such policies are dynamically time inconsistent in the absence of a commitment technology or reliable reputation effects. It is understandable that the public may entertain doubts about such long-horizon commitments.

The discussion in the previous section suggests that, given the current outlook, strategies to provide additional stimulus would be consistent with achieving outcomes better aligned with the assumed long-run policy goals. Nevertheless, such "optimal" policies might be viewed as theoretical references of limited usefulness in Committee communications, because they are both complex and model-dependent, and because they do not reveal how the Committee would respond to changes in the economic outlook.

In this section, we consider strategies that the policymaker could potentially implement to augment simple policy rules. In particular, we study threshold policies by which the monetary authority commits itself not to depart from the effective lower bound, notwithstanding the prescriptions of its simple monetary policy rule, *at least* until a threshold condition is satisfied, *either* the unemployment rate drops below a certain level *or* the projection for inflation rises above a certain level. Threshold strategies of this nature may provide one or both of two possible benefits. The first is the clarification and reinforcement of the intentions of monetary policy as encompassed within the simple rule. In worlds in which knowledge of the extant policy rule cannot be taken as given, and hence the benefits of rational expectations are not assured, the use of the *enhanced forward guidance* we discuss here can be sizable, even if they are hard to quantify. In this sense, threshold strategies provide much of the same benefits that date-based forward guidance does, except that because threshold policies are *state-based forward guidance*, in principle, they need not be adjusted continuously as the economy evolves over time. Instead, private agents can adjust their beliefs of the likely date of policy firming for themselves

---

[29] See, for instance, Orphanides and Wieland (2000), Kato and Nishiyama (2005), and Adam and Billi (2007).

as the economy gets closer (or further) to crossing a threshold value; to the extent that such forward guidance improves investors' understanding of the Committee's reaction function, such guidance can make it more likely that investors' responses to incoming data will move medium- and longer-term rates in a way that is consistent with the Committee's thinking about the likely future path of short-term rates. Second, to the extent that the stating of thresholds can serve as a commitment device, properly designed threshold strategies can provide additional stimulus that comes from the "lower for longer" *conditional commitment* to maintain accommodative policy for longer than policymakers would in a discretionary equilibrium. This forbearance from the prescriptions of the accompanying simple rule captures aspects of the "history dependent" strategies that characterize the optimal policy under commitment. According to this argument, if the Committee were to announce, say, its intention to keep short-term interest rates near zero until certain economic conditions were met (i.e., introducing thresholds), private agents would be confident that the Committee would indeed do so on the expectation that the Committee would be unwilling to suffer the loss in reputation associated with a failure to follow through on its pledge. As a result, the stated policy would be more likely to shift the public's expectations for short-term interest rates, inflation, and other factors in the desired directions.

Following this strategy, the policymaker might choose to specify thresholds for the inflation rate and unemployment rate to clarify conditions governing the onset of tightening. In addition, forward guidance could be used to clarify the strategy the central bank intends to follow after it initiates tightening. In this vein, the policymaker might emphasize that its intended exit strategy embeds key features of the optimal policy; hence, such guidance could be interpreted as consistent with "flexible inflation targeting under commitment." Specifically, the policymaker could indicate that it would permit inflation to rise modestly and temporary, above its 2 percent mandate, on the grounds that a period of higher inflation, given a nominal rate fixed at the effective lower bound, would bring real interest rates down and hence stimulate demand, thereby allowing the unemployment rate to decline below the estimated natural rate as the economic recovery progressed.

We now explore the potential macroeconomic effects of adopting a threshold strategy using simulations of our model. We consider both the macroeconomic implications of setting thresholds at different levels and the importance of what monetary policy does after a threshold is crossed. In light of the highly uncertain outlook for real activity and inflation, we next investigate the likely performance of a threshold strategy in the face of unexpected economic developments, based on the sort of shocks that have hit the economy over the last 40 years. The choice of a threshold pair, and the associated choice of the post-crossing policy rule, may have an important bearing on expectations formation and economic performance. For example, if the Committee were to choose a relatively low threshold for the unemployment rate and a high threshold for inflation, it would, in effect, be signaling an intention to be persistently more accommodative than would be suggested by historical experience or by most simple policy rules.

Our analysis starts with the assumption that the public currently expects the economy to evolve along the lines shown in the solid black line of Figure 6 which corresponds to the outcomes obtained under the inertial Taylor rule. We then consider the consequences of an announcement that the FOMC intends to follow a threshold strategy. For example, the yellow dot-dashed line shows one particular threshold pairing in which the federal funds rate is held near zero until *either* the unemployment rate falls below 6.5 percent, *or* core PCE inflation over the medium term is projected to exceed 2.5 percent.[30] We employ a projection-based inflation threshold in order to reduce the possibility that transitory fluctuations in inflation related to energy or other shocks could lead to the threshold being crossed. In addition, the simulations assume that once either threshold condition is crossed, the federal funds rate then follows the prescriptions of the inertial Taylor rule. It is important to understand that the switch in policy upon crossing a threshold does not imply an immediate increase in the federal funds rate; rather a crossing merely implies that forbearance of the policy rule's prescriptions comes to an end.[31] Importantly, the public is assumed to understand the announced change in policy and to view it as fully credible.

Under the 6.5/2.5 percent threshold pair, the federal funds rate begins to rise from its effective lower bound six quarters after the prescription without thresholds, gradually climbs to 3 percent by 2018, and after that eventually rises above the trajectory without thresholds. In other words, the threshold strategy moves monetary policy away from that of the unadorned inertial Taylor rule, the black line, some distance toward the optimal commitment policy, the dot-dashed purple line. As might be expected, this threshold pair gives better economic outcomes than the rule without thresholds but falls considerably short of the performance of the (possibly infeasible) commitment strategy. The remaining lines in the figure show the policy prescriptions and economic effects of other threshold pairings, where each pair holds the inflation threshold constant at 2.5 percent and varies the unemployment threshold. Summarizing these results, for this baseline, model and simple policy rule, reducing the unemployment threshold improves measured economic performance until the unemployment threshold reaches 5.5 percent; a further reduction in the threshold to 5.0 percent, however, reduces welfare, as the control of inflation becomes notably less precise.

Figure 6 also illustrates the potential implications of altering market expectations regarding the behavior of the funds rate *after* firming begins, again conditional on the baseline outlook for real activity and inflation. As the figure shows, late departures in the federal funds rate that occur with lower unemployment thresholds are associated with steeper subsequent climbs in the federal funds rate. Because current economic conditions are determined in large part by expectations of the entire future path of the real federal funds rate, these sharp climbs offset, to some degree, some of the stimulative effects of deferred firming. A post-lower-bound policy that is more gradual would produce a larger initial boost in aggregate demand, albeit possibly at some cost. This result highlights the potential importance of guidance about the Committee's intentions for the stance of monetary policy after the onset of tightening.

Figure 7 repeats the exercise of Figure 6, except that this time it is the unemployment threshold that is held constant, at 6.5 percent, and the inflation threshold is varied from 1.5 percent to 3.0

---

[30] Specifically, the inflation threshold is defined in terms of the eight-quarter-ahead projection of the trailing four-quarter rate of core PCE price inflation as forecast by the model. In the absence of future shocks, the inflation forecast will equal the actual future rate of inflation generated in the simulation and will be consistent with the current and projected future path for policy.

[31] Other assumptions are possible, of course. One could assume that policy reverts to the simple rule gradually over time, for example. The approach taken here has the advantage of simplicity.

percent. In this instance, varying the inflation threshold has comparatively small implications—and indeed over some range, no material implications—for economic outcomes.[32,33]

Our analysis to this point has examined how threshold strategies influence real activity, inflation, and interest rates under baseline conditions. We now broaden the analysis by evaluating macroeconomic performance under threshold strategies in response to a wide range of economic disturbances. To do this, we run stochastic simulations of the model, an approach that allows us to construct probability distributions for future economic conditions. To save space, we focus on results for the inertial Taylor rule.

The hollow bars in the various panels of Figure 8 repeat what we showed in one panel of Figure 2, namely the distribution of the dates of the first increase in the funds rate for the inertial Taylor rule without thresholds. The blue bars, lying on top of the hollow bars, show how the distribution is shifted by the implementation of the threshold strategy. The left-hand column shows the effects of varying the unemployment threshold, holding constant the inflation threshold at its baseline value of 2.5 percent; the right-hand column varies the inflation threshold, holding the unemployment threshold at its baseline value of 6.5 percent. The values of the unemployment threshold have an important bearing on the date that the federal funds rate departs from the effective lower bound, as all of the thresholds shown lead to a substantial deferral of first tightening. At the same time, it is worth noting that while the strategy ameliorates some possible apprehension on the part of private agents regarding what could be an inappropriately early firming, the cost of this is a general reduction in the predictability of firming dates and an associated decline in the effectiveness of date-based forward guidance that might serve as a complement to threshold strategies.

The effects of varying the inflation threshold are less impressive but still noteworthy. Even a very low threshold rate of 1.5 percent for inflation shifts the distribution noticeably. Indeed, the fact that the choice of the inflation threshold does affect the likely date of firming in a stochastic environment, whereas under the baseline scenario it had little to no effect, stands as an important reminder that monetary policy design, in the broad sense of that term, needs to consider a range of economic outlooks.

Table 2 presents some statistics on our stochastic simulation runs. Comparing columns [1] and [2] shows that there can be a substantial delay between the date a threshold is crossed and the date of initial tightening. Columns [3] and [4] note how changes in the threshold pairings alter the likelihood that one threshold or another will be crossed, in ways that one might expect. This clearly shows that thresholds are effective in shifting the date of firming; however, it says nothing about whether they deliver favorable economic outcomes. The remaining columns address this question by providing some estimates of economic performance. In particular, column [7] shows the proportion of stochastic draws for which the use of the threshold policy gives better economic performance than does the policy rule without thresholds, as measured by the same loss function we used in constructing the optimal policies above. As can be seen, the

---

[32] We warn the reader that this result is not general. There are combinations of models, baselines and policy rules for which the adjustment of the inflation threshold would have a material effect on measured losses.

[33] Measured using the same loss function as was used to construct the optimal policies, the rankings of the various threshold policies, with the inertial Taylor rule, for the baseline scenario as of 2018:Q4 are, from lowest loss to highest: commitment > discretion > 5.5/2.5 > 5.0/2.5 > 6.0/2.5 > 6.5/2.5 = 6.5/2.0 = 6.5/3.0 > 6.5/1.5 > no thresholds, where the first number in a pair is the unemployment threshold and the second is the inflation threshold.

proportion of draws that feature improvements in welfare is high to very high, regardless of the threshold pair. In short, thresholds work. At the same time, there is some evidence of tradeoffs between performance on average and performance in the tail cases as can be seen in comparing losses for the 5.0/2.5 thresholds to those with the other threshold pairs. The 5.0/2.5 pair, shown in the second line of the table, renders the lowest loss, on average and at the median, but the share of draws for which welfare is improved is notably lower than for other pairs. This finding hints at certain fragility in expected improvements in welfare as policy forbearance becomes more aggressive.[34]

While thresholds work on average, performance can vary significantly depending on conditions. Examining those draws for which marked improvements in economic performance are realized with thresholds and comparing those to the identical scenario without thresholds is instructive. Draws for which the effects of the 6.5/2.5 threshold pair are salutary tend to have relatively high realized inflation in the early going of the scenario—such that policy rules without thresholds have a tendency to prescribe liftoff—but not so high and not so persistent that the projection–based inflation threshold is crossed. Thus, the thresholds in these draws tend to produce a substantial degree of policy forbearance as measured by the length of time for which liftoff is deferred. Particularly large improvements also arise when a sequence of real-side shocks brings about an increase in the unemployment rate, in contrast to the downward trend in the baseline, as these are the circumstances in which "staying lower for longer" is particularly beneficial. Not surprisingly these draws often feature regret in the sense of a return to the effective lower bound within four quarters in the version without thresholds.[35]

Finally, in Figure 9, we reconsider the probability of return to the effective lower bound, following initial departure, this time for our threshold strategies. Just as we saw that even mildly restrictive thresholds may have a material effect on probabilities of leaving the lower bound, so too do they have an effect on the likelihood of returning to the lower bound. As the figure shows, the introduction of thresholds reduces the sensitivity of the inertial Taylor rule to modest changes in economic conditions because it is less likely that the rule will respond to what turns out to be a purely transitory improvement in real activity or in inflation and deleteriously call for policy to begin to tighten, only to find that the policy rate needs to return to the effective lower bound shortly thereafter.[36]

The likelihood of regret and the associated difficulty in predicting firming dates underscores the communication challenges associated with the use of threshold strategies. Ideally, thresholds would be cast in terms of readily verifiable and easily understandable measures. However the variables that matter in economic models—objects like output gaps and unemployment gaps—

---

[34] Remarkably, the key result that welfare is improved by the use of thresholds in a high to very high proportion of draws holds up almost as well when the model is simulated assuming that agents form expectations using a small-scale VAR model, rather than model-consistent expectations. Details of these simulations are available from the authors upon request.

[35] It seems reasonable to expect that a baseline in which the proportion of threshold crossings that arise from crossing the inflation threshold is higher would produce more draws where thresholds produce large gains. We have not formally tested this proposition, however.

[36] The effect of thresholds is more substantial in terms of both the deferral of policy firming and the likelihood of returning to the zero lower bound for static policy rules like the Taylor (1993) and Taylor (1999) rules because as we have already shown, these rules tend to produce early firming and these often turn out to be deleterious for economic performance. For example, the 6.5/2.5 threshold pair improves welfare in 95 percent of draws for the Taylor (1999) rule.

are harder for the public to understand and, in any case, are often only narrow proxies for broader concepts of "excess demand" in the minds of policymakers. The probability that a threshold pair would need to be recalibrated owing to shifts in, say, labor market conditions that are not well captured solely by fluctuations in the unemployment rate—driven by movements in the labor force participation rate, for example—is not something that can be safely ignored. Broadly similar communications challenges arise owing to the use of *projected* inflation used in place of realized inflation because of the volatility of the latter, buffeted as it is by significant but transitory shocks.

Summary

Our examination of the possible benefits of employing threshold-based forward guidance suggests that thresholds, if understood and seen as credible, can significantly improve economic outcomes. Of course, such guidance could also be delivered by providing the expected date of the first increase in the federal funds rate given the economic outlook. However, as we saw, that approach would likely require a number of changes in the date as the outlook evolved, which could be confusing to the public and undermine the credibility of the forward guidance. The analysis also suggests that guidance regarding the federal funds rate after it is first increased from its effective lower bound can also improve performance. Indeed, the FOMC arguably has included such guidance, albeit qualitatively, in its recent postmeeting statements, which have indicated that "when the Committee decides to begin to remove policy accommodation, it will take a balanced approach consistent with its longer-run goals of maximum employment and inflation of 2 percent."

B.2. Large-scale asset purchases

As with its forward guidance regarding the federal funds rate, the Committee has changed the way it communicates its asset purchase decisions over time as it has gained experience with the tool. The first announcements of purchases indicated the expected total amount of purchases and a timeframe over which they would be conducted, but also clearly noted that the Committee could make changes to the program as conditions evolved. Indeed the purchases of agency debt securities in the first LSAP program were reduced somewhat in size in response to market strains, and the maturity extension program (which involved purchases of longer-term securities coupled with equal-sized sales of shorter-maturity securities) was extended for six months after the initial anticipated ending date and ended up totaling $600 billion, rather than the $400 billion initially announced.[37]

---

[37] In this subsection, we do not directly address the macroeconomic effects of balance sheet policies. There is a substantial recent research literature that has tried to quantify the effects of balance sheet policies on asset pricing (see, for instance, D'Amico *et al.* (2012) and Krishnamurthy and Vissing-Jorgensen (2011, 2013) for recent new evidence and a review of this literature). In addition, there is some evidence that purchases have provided appreciable stimulus to real activity as well helped to check disinflationary pressures (see, for instance, Chung *et al.*, 2012). An important lesson of this analysis is that the overall stance of monetary policy has been more stimulative than would be suggested by the level of the short-term interest rate alone. In such a situation, gauging the appropriateness of the overall stance of monetary policy by comparing the level of the nominal federal funds rate to, say, the prescriptions of some simple instrument rule may be problematic.

By contrast, the current purchase program did not feature a fixed expected size. Instead, the Committee indicated that the purchases would continue until "the outlook for the labor market" improved "substantially" in a context of price stability. This approach is somewhat similar to the use of thresholds for the forward guidance for the federal funds rate in that it describes the economic conditions under which the purchases would end. However, the language employed is less specific, not providing numerical thresholds for particular economic variables. One possible reason for the more limited specificity is uncertainty regarding the efficacy and costs associated with additional purchases. Indeed, since asset purchases are such a new policy tool, the historical record for judging such effects is limited. Taking account of this uncertainty, the Committee has stated clearly that its decisions on the size and composition of purchases will depend on its ongoing assessment of the efficacy and costs of purchases.[38] While a complete analysis of the policy implications of uncertainty about the efficacy and costs of purchases is beyond the scope of this paper, a simple, static model of asset purchases can be used to illustrate the tradeoffs involved in such decisions.

Balancing the efficacy and costs of securities purchases: A simple model [39]

We start by assuming that the macroeconomic benefits, B, of securities purchases, S, are a function of the amount of purchases and their efficacy, e, where efficacy captures the size of the effect of a given amount of purchases on longer-term interest rates and broader financial conditions:

$$Benefits = B(eS - H)$$

These benefits include increased employment as well as inflation that are closer to the Committee's longer-run goal. (We assume that policymakers start from a situation in which they would like to provide additional monetary accommodation, but they are unable to do so because of the effective lower bound on the federal funds rate.) These benefits of the purchases are assumed to be countered by headwinds, H, generated by private sector deleveraging, tight lending standards, fiscal contraction, and the like. For simplicity, we assume that the benefits of purchases are increasing in purchases and efficacy—that is, B' is positive—and that the marginal benefits are declining in purchases and efficacy—that is, B'' is negative.

We assume that the costs associated with securities purchases, C, are summarized by:

$$Costs = C(S)$$

These costs include possible effects on market functioning, potential implications for exit and consequent effects on expected inflation, potential implications for Federal Reserve income, and concerns about financial stability.[40] For simplicity, we assume that these costs are increasing in the level of securities purchases—that is, C' is positive—and that marginal costs are also increasing in the level of purchases—that is, C'' is also positive.

In this simple, static setup, policymakers want to choose the level of purchases in order to maximize their net benefits:

---

[38] See, for example, the statement issued after the August FOMC meeting.
[39] We thank Ben Bernanke for suggesting this approach.
[40] For a discussion of these possible costs and risks, see Bernanke (2012b).

Net Benefits $= B(eS - H) - C(S)$

The first-order condition for the optimal level of purchases, S^*, is given by:

$B'(eS^* - H)e = C'(S^*)$

And, given our assumptions, the second-order condition for a maximum is satisfied.

Implications

There are three straightforward implications of this simple model that would seem likely to generalize to a larger model. First, if policymakers come to believe that the marginal cost of additional purchases is lower (higher) than previously believed, then the optimal level of securities purchases, S^*, will be higher (lower). Second, if the headwinds, H, prove to be larger (smaller) than expected then it is appropriate for purchases to be increased (decreased). However, one can show that the adjustment in purchases will not be enough to fully offset the change in headwinds. For example, if the headwinds increase, then it will be optimal to increase purchases, but by a somewhat smaller amount than would be required to offset the added headwinds because the marginal cost of additional purchases increases as purchases rise.

Finally, the model can be used to assess the implications for policy of a change in policymakers' assessment of the efficacy of purchases, e. In general, a change in e has two offsetting effects. For example, with reduced efficacy, the total amount of accommodation provided by a given level of purchases is reduced, increasing the benefits of additional accommodation. However, the accommodation provided by an additional dollar of securities purchases is smaller with the reduction in e, implying a smaller gain in relation to the marginal cost of the purchases.

These two effects can be seen in the context of a simple parametric example. Assume that the benefits of securities purchases are given by:

$$B(eS - H) = -\frac{1}{2}(eS - H - A)^2$$

where A is the level of monetary accommodation that would yield the best macroeconomic outcomes in the absence of the costs and risks associated with securities purchases. Also assume that the costs associated with securities purchases are given by:

$C(S) = kS^2$

where k is a positive constant.

In this case, the optimal level of securities purchases is given by:

$$S^* = \frac{e(A+H)}{2k + e^2}$$

And the effect of a change in e on S^* is given by:

$$\frac{dS^*}{de} = S^* \left[\frac{1}{e} - \frac{2e}{2k+e^2}\right]$$

So in this case, the optimal level of securities purchases increases in response to an increase in efficacy if e is small, but it declines if e is large.

In practice, policymakers would face uncertainty about the level of costs and efficacy, which would likely lead to a reduced level of purchases, at least for a time. The reduction would reflect both the direct effect of uncertain policy multipliers, as in Brainard (1967), and also the fact that the Committee would learn about efficacy and costs over time. Thus, the desired pace and level of purchases would depend in part on the Committee's ongoing assessment of their efficacy and costs, as noted in the Committee's post meeting statements since the start of the current purchase program.

In our discussion of asset purchases, we have left aside their possible effect on the impact of forward guidance. In practice, there is some evidence that purchases, by suggesting that the Federal Reserve has "skin in the game" may help to make forward guidance regarding the federal funds rate more credible to market participants (see, e.g., Woodford (2012b); Bauer and Rudebusch (2011)). Thus, the mere announcement of promises of future funds rate actions might be insufficient to successfully obtain the benefits today of the planned policy. In that case, a visible action, like the expansion of the balance sheet, may help to convince the public that the Federal Reserve will carry through on its promised degree of policy accommodation. If this is the case, decisions on forward guidance and purchases would have to be linked and modeling would need to take account of the mix of such policies employed to assess the likely macroeconomic outcomes.

B.3. Unconventional policies at foreign central banks

While the discussion thus far has focused on the recent experience of the Federal Reserve, a number of foreign central banks have faced policy challenges similar to those faced by the Federal Reserve and have taken similar steps with regard to nontraditional monetary policy tools in response. Thus, our analysis has broader application. Table 3 summarizes unconventional monetary policies implemented by major foreign central banks to provide extra support to economic activity after reaching the effective lower bound on short-term policy rates.

Large-scale asset purchase programs

In October 2010, the Bank of Japan (BOJ) launched an "Asset Purchase Program" (APP) whose size reached ¥101 trillion (more than 20 percent of GDP) by December 2012. The program covered a wide range of both public and private securities. Purchases were unsterilized and concentrated in relatively short-term securities. In April 2013, the BOJ replaced the APP by a new "Quantitative and Qualitative Easing" program that should lead to a doubling of the BOJ's balance sheet to about 60 percent of GDP by late 2014. The new program will significantly extend the average remaining maturity of Japanese government bonds purchased, which should also help increase downward pressure on longer-term rates, and it will also boost holdings of exchange-traded funds and Japanese real estate investment trusts.

In the United Kingdom, the Bank of England (BOE) has acquired £375 billion (equal to about 25 percent of GDP) in domestic assets through the injection of central bank reserves. Purchases took place in two phases: March 2009 to January 2010 and October 2011 to October 2012. Gilts represent over 99 percent of the assets purchased, with corporate bonds and commercial paper accounting for the residual.

The European Central Bank (ECB) has operated four programs of outright asset purchases on a fully sterilized basis. Under the "Securities Market Programme," the ECB bought €208.7 billion in peripheral euro-area securities. The program operated from May 2010 to August 2012 and was replaced by the Outright Monetary Transactions (OMTs) program. OMTs, which have yet to be activated, allow the ECB to purchase shorter-term sovereign debt of euro-area countries conditional on these countries' participation in a European Financial Stability Facility/European Stability Mechanism macroeconomic adjustment program. Finally, the ECB ran two covered bond programs between mid-2009 and late 2012 with cumulative purchases of €76 billion (¾ percent of GDP). Between late 2009 and early 2012, the ECB also conducted a series of one-year and three-year long-term refinancing operations (LTROs) on a fixed-rate, full-allotment basis. Its three-year LTROs in December 2011 and February 2012 allotted €489 billion (5¼ percent of GDP) and €530 billion (5½ percent of GDP), respectively. Although refinancing operations are typically not classified under large-scale asset purchase programs, the ECB's exceptionally sizeable and unsterilized LTROs have been credited for some of the same positive effects on financial markets, notably a reduction in peripheral yields (Rogers, Scotti and Wright (2013)).

Forward guidance

In March 2013, the U.K. Treasury mandated the BOE to assess the merits of using intermediate activity and inflation thresholds. As a result of this deliberation, the BOE announced on August 7, 2013, its intention "not to raise Bank Rate from its current level of 0.5% at least until the Labour Force Survey headline measure of the unemployment rate has fallen to a threshold of 7%." The guidance is subject to provisos, labeled "knockout conditions:" that the Monetary Policy Committee expects inflation to exceed its 2 percent target by more than 0.5 percent 18 to 24 months ahead, that market participants' medium-term inflation expectations are no longer sufficiently well anchored, and that Financial Policy Committee judges that the stance of monetary policy poses a significant threat to financial stability.[41] Thus, the approach taken by the BOE is similar to that ultimately taken by the Federal Reserve. Even earlier, in June, the BOE had sought to guide interest rates in response to the rise in U.K. yields in sympathy with U.S. yields after the June 2013 FOMC meeting, stating that "the implied rise in the expected future path of Bank Rate was not warranted by the recent developments in the domestic economy."

Both the BOJ and the ECB have provided more limited forward guidance. In conjunction with the launch of its APP in October 2010, the BOJ declared its intention to maintain zero interest rates until it judged that price stability was in sight on the basis of its "medium- to long-term understanding of price stability (i.e. 1 percent)." On July 4, 2013, the ECB added the following language to the statement that follows its monetary policy decisions: "The Governing Council expects the key ECB interest rates to remain at present or lower levels for an extended period of time. This expectation is based on the overall subdued outlook for inflation extending into the medium term, given the broad-based weakness in the real economy and subdued monetary dynamics."

Other notable actions

---

[41] Importantly, the BOE stated that there is "no presumption that breaching any of these knockouts would lead to an immediate increase in the Bank Rate or sale of assets." Thus the knockout conditions are thresholds, not triggers.

In addition to forward guidance and asset purchases, some central banks have pursued programs intended to bolster lending to the private sector. For example, the BOE and U.K. Treasury announced a "Funding for Lending Scheme" in June 2012 that was designed to provide an incentive for banks to boost their lending to the nonfinancial sector. Under the program, participants can swap a wide range of assets for Treasury Bills, which improves their liquidity positions and should help them borrow in private funding markets at lower rates than they would otherwise be able to by using the Bills as collateral.

Similarly, since June 2010, the BOJ has implemented a series of initiatives to support lending to the real sector through a ¥5.5 trillion (1¼ percent of GDP) "Loan Support Program." The largest initiative, the "Growth-Supporting Funding Facility," is fully operated by the BOJ, with its staff reviewing the eligibility of individual loans and monitoring their progress.

II. Questions Regarding Monetary Policy Frameworks Raised by the Financial Crisis and its Aftermath

Not surprisingly, the financial crisis and the ensuing, severe recession have raised additional questions about the most appropriate framework for monetary policy. In this section, we explore two of these questions. First, we consider whether policymakers could improve economic performance by changing their objectives. In particular, it has been suggested that introducing a higher (permanent) target rate of inflation could provide more of a buffer against the effective lower bound constraint on nominal interest rates and so allow for improved economic outcomes (Summers (1991), and more recently, Blanchard *et al.* (2010)). Alternatively, as we discussed above, given the benefits that can be achieved when the nominal interest rate is at its lower bound from a policy that is history-dependent, some have suggested that central banks should target the level of nominal GDP (Woodford (2012b)). The second question raised by the crisis and its aftermath that we consider here is how monetary policy and financial stability policy frameworks should be integrated. The crisis has led central banks to move financial stability policy back to the forefront of their responsibilities alongside monetary policy, but significant work remains to assess the appropriate approach to the two goals (see Bernanke (2013c)).

A. Possible Benefits of a Change in Objective

As we will discuss below, a key issue regarding a possible change in the central bank's objective is the importance of credibility for any change in regime to be successful, especially during a period when short-term rates are constrained by the lower bound and so, conventional policy instruments are constrained. Achieving such credibility could be difficult, and either change in objective might be seen by financial market participants and wage and price setters as either confusing or not credible, raising significant communications issues that could undermine the economic benefits of the change.[42]

---

[42] Indeed, to the best of our knowledge, only once has an inflation targeting country raised its target without also changing the targeted variable. That was New Zealand in 1997 when it widened its inflation band from 0-to-2

An additional, related complication is that there is remarkably little experience with either price-level targeting or nominal-income targeting. The one clear-cut historical precedent for price-level targeting is when Sweden abandoned the gold standard in 1931 and attempted instead to maintain the September 1931 price level (Fregert and Jonung (1999)). The policy was associated with Sweden's avoidance of the deflation that plagued countries still operating under the gold standard, but whether there is much to take from this for modern times is questionable. No country has formally targeted nominal income.

A.1. A permanent increase in the target rate of inflation?

There is a substantial literature on the costs of inflation, one that is too large (and too well known) for us to survey here. We take it for granted that prior to the crisis the case for defining "price stability" as steady-state inflation near two percent for broad indexes of prices was a compelling one, in part because of the effects of the effective lower bound on interest rates. [43] Thus, a more interesting issue, from our point of view, is what case can be made for engineering a permanent increase in the inflation rate under current conditions; that is, under circumstances in which the effective lower bound is binding, inflation is below its current target, and the economy is likely in excess supply.

In the stylized world of textbook rational expectations models, the question almost answers itself: a credible increase in the target rate of inflation would reduce real interest rates, relax the effective lower bound constraint, and thereby help conventional monetary policy to regain its effectiveness. Moreover, it would also reduce the asymmetric effects of negative shocks on the economy. But reality introduces a number of practical concerns. After all, if policy were as credible as textbooks assume, inflation would arguably already be at its (current) target. Indeed, the question of the origins of rational expectations—and policy credibility—is a valid one. The literature shows that a rational expectations equilibrium can arise out of a process of learning, provided that a given policy is in place long enough for private agents to learn it (see, e.g., Evans and Honkapohja (2001)). Whether agents can be expected to come to understand a change in a policy rule, such as a change in the target rate of inflation, and form a rational expectation of the implications of that rule without experiencing the regime beforehand, is an open question.

Figure 10 provides one illustration of these issues. The purple dot-dashed line shows the effects of a credible, once-and-for-all increase in the target rate of inflation to three percent, under the inertial Taylor rule. Compared with the baseline case introduced in Figure 1 and shown here as the red dashed line, where the target remains at two percent, the higher path for inflation induces a more rapid increase in the nominal federal funds rate. Real interest rates, however, are lower than in the baseline, so the unemployment rate falls considerably more rapidly than in the baseline, as shown in the lower-left panel.

However, this result depends on rational expectations and the credibility of the change in objective. In an alternative simulation, shown by the black solid lines, we assume that while

---

percent to 0-to-3 percent. New Zealand went on to experience poor economic performance for a time, albeit for reasons having nothing to do with the change in target.

[43] Recently, Coibion et al. (2012) explicitly study, in the context of a modern macroeconomic New Keynesian model, the effect of the zero lower bound on the optimal inflation rate, and they find that, for plausible calibrations, an inflation target around 2 percent is robustly optimal.

expectations in financial markets continue to be rational in the usual sense of that word, the expectations of agents in non-financial markets are formed using a small-scale VAR model.[44] This assumption means that the "free lunch" of a credible increase in the *perceived* target rate of inflation from the mere announcement of a higher target is circumscribed. In this instance, part of the increase in nominal bond rates observed by non-financial agents is perceived as a real phenomenon, leading to a reduction in expenditures and prices in the short run. The monetary authority responds to these "headwinds" by deferring departure from the effective lower bound. The deferral in tightening notwithstanding, the improvement in the real economy proceeds at pace that is initially even slower than in the baseline and inflation is lower than in the baseline for a time, as the lower panels show.

However, there is nothing to say that the pessimistic scenario portrayed by the black solid line is more likely than the credible rational expectations scenario. And other possibilities come easily to mind, including ones where the perceived target rate of inflation overshoots the central bank's actual target, obliging a subsequent costly contraction. What these scenarios do effectively highlight, however, is how critical expectations formation is for the efficacy of policy at the effective lower bound.[45]

A.2. Nominal GDP targeting

In an earlier section we discussed the features of optimal policies, in particular their propensity to promise "lower for longer" as a funds rate prescription and to generate a modest overshooting of inflation of its long-run target. However, such optimal policies are of limited usefulness, partly because they are complex and model dependent, but also because they do not reveal how the Committee would respond to changes in the economic outlook. We also discussed how simple policy rules could be augmented with thresholds in order to go at least part of the way toward optimal commitment policies and thereby generate results closer to policymakers' goals. In this section, we consider another strategy, the adoption of an intermediate target for nominal income.

As recently reemphasized by Woodford (2012b), pursuing a nominal income *level* target implicitly aims to reverse past inflation shortfalls rather than let bygones be bygones, thereby inducing a form of history dependence that moves policy a step closer to the optimal policy with commitment under the effective lower bound in the context of NKB models. Under this approach, the Committee would choose a target path for nominal income, y_N^*, and commit to using available instruments to minimize the gap between nominal income and this target (or a forecast of the gap) over time. It is useful to decompose the nominal income target into a price-level component and an activity component (that is, $y_N^* = p^* y^*$, where p^* is the price-level target, and y^* is the real output target). Importantly, nominal income targeting does not necessarily require agreement on an estimate of the output gap, as different views on the output gap would simply correspond to different implied paths for the price level over the medium term to achieve a given nominal income target. Once the nominal income gap is closed, however,

---

[44] Indeed, VAR-based expectations are a standard assumption for simulations of the FRB/US model, although rational expectations are also commonly assumed. See Brayton and Tinsley (1996) for a discussion.

[45] Ascari and Sbordone (2013) theoretically discuss similar issues to emphasize that a permanently higher inflation will be associated with a more unstable economy and will tend to destabilize inflation expectations.

such a strategy would imply similar outlooks for inflation and economic growth in the longer run, assuming broadly similar views regarding the growth rate of potential GDP going forward. Just as the choice of a target path is a major ingredient of price-level targeting, the choice of a target path for nominal income is important for nominal-income targeting. A simple extrapolation of the price component of the target at a 2 percent rate is a natural choice; with regard to the target path for output, a reasonable course would be to base the path for y^* on current estimates and forecasts of the economy's potential output, and then to update the projections on a periodic basis.

One appealing feature of a nominal income target in the U.S. setting is that it explicitly recognizes both sides of the dual mandate. Indeed, the equal weights on the price-level gap and output gap would be consistent with a similar degree of concern for both objectives. A nominal income target could also provide effective forward guidance to reinforce market perceptions about the strength of the Committee's desire to keep interest rates low for an extended period, given that the gap between nominal income and target could initially be quite large. Of course, the Committee would need to make it clear to the public that the nominal income targeting framework is not simply a cover for engineering a temporary or perhaps permanent rise in the inflation target; to this end, the Committee would want to demonstrate that the implicit gap in resource utilization underlying the initial nominal-income gap is reasonable.

Figure 10 illustrates how nominal-income targeting might move policy a step closer, compared with the inertial Taylor strategy, to the optimal policy under our baseline scenario. The delayed firming from the effective lower bound under nominal income targeting —the green dashed lines in the figure—like the commitment strategy, leads to a sharper reduction in the unemployment rate than under the inertial Taylor rule. This rapid real-side improvement is facilitated by a moderate overshooting of inflation of its target, which reduces the real rate despite no movement, initially, in the nominal funds rate. There is a cost, however: Nominal income targeting engenders a period of excess demand toward the end of the decade, something that the commitment strategy, if it were feasible, would not produce. The beneficial effects of nominal income targeting arise because of its self-correcting nature: As the shortfall in activity lowers nominal income directly and through lower prices, policy is expected to remain accommodative for longer (top left panel), thereby providing additional stimulus—by causing the unemployment rate to substantially undershoot its equilibrium level.

The demands on the public's attention and comprehension imposed by nominal income targeting are arguably more severe than they are for other rule-based regimes. The implications of revisions to the data are a pertinent example. Any monetary policy regime that depends, at least in part, on an informed public, runs the risk of sowing confusion and error when the data that underlie prior communications are revised. However, whereas a revision, say, to historical inflation is unlikely to change either the objective or, in any serious way, the tactics of an inflation targeting central bank, this is not necessarily the case for a central bank that targets the level of nominal income. The efficacy of such a regime requires that the private sector knows what the initial discrepancy is between the level of nominal income and its target level; without such knowledge, the benefits of people's expectation that the price-level gap will be closed over time will not be realized. But this initial gap is subject to revision in the source data for nominal income. Figure 11 shows the pattern of revisions to the reported level of nominal income for selected vintages over the period since the deepening of the financial crisis in 2008. So, for example, the black line, labeled "2007:Q4" shows how estimates of the level nominal income *for*

2007:Q4 changed with the vintage of the data, indexed by the x axis. In each case shown, we index the initial level of rebased to 100 for ease of comparison. As can be seen, the level of nominal income has been subject to significant revision, generally of two to four percent and sometimes more.[46] That such revisions can have substantial implications is demonstrated in Figure 12. The green dashed line is our nominal-income targeting scenario, repeated from Figure 10; that scenario is conditional on an initial nominal-income-level gap of about -6 percent. The red dotted line shows a similar scenario, but with an initial gap that is 4 percentage points smaller, in line with the pattern of historical revisions. As can be seen, the policy implications of such a revision are substantial. Of course, one could, at least in principle, simply revise the target path for nominal income to offset the upward revision in the data. But while it may well be beneficial to do so, the demands on private agents' attention span and comprehension of such changes should not be taken lightly.

To illustrate further the dependence of nominal income level targeting on expectations formation, we consider in Figure 13 a case where expectations of future prices and output are taken to be bounded rational; in particular, we assume that agents, instead of believing wholly and unreservedly in the predictions of the model, form expectations of future events using a small-scale VAR, a model that eschews the cross-equation restrictions of our base-case model. As the red dotted line in the figure shows, VAR-based expectations allow a protracted period in which inflation overshoots its long-run objective owing to the introduction of an extrapolative element in expectations by this departure from model-consistent expectations. In this instance, expectations are not "well anchored" as is generally the case under rational expectations, so that a period of persistently high inflation induces households, firms, and investors to mark up their expectations of inflation, touching off what amounts to a wage-price spiral. Monetary policy is forced to cope with this spiral by more tightening than is called for in the baseline toward the end of the period shown.

A.3. Communications challenges

In short, both a higher inflation objective and nominal GDP targeting could, if communicated clearly and found to be credible, improve economic outcomes. But a number of communications challenges make such changes in framework less likely to be successful in practice.

Most important, the effectiveness of such changes depends on influencing the public's beliefs about the policy strategy likely to prevail as much as five years or more ahead. Accordingly, the ability of policymakers to influence expectations hinges on the public's belief that the strategy will be followed for many years, including well after the point at which the unemployment rate has returned to a level consistent with full employment. But the public may be skeptical about such long-horizon commitments. The benefits of these strategies are frontloaded while the costs are incurred later, providing an incentive to renege. Moreover, the adoption of one of these strategies might not be seen as credible because the Committee cannot really bind its successors.

More broadly, the public may not understand the change in policy framework and so may be confused about the central bank's intentions. The change could well be seen as policymakers backing away from their commitment to low and stable inflation, thereby unanchoring inflation

---

[46] Revisions to nominal income were even larger in the late 1990s.

expectations and so limiting the ability of policymakers to use policy to counter adverse aggregate demand shocks without causing a sharp run-up in inflation expectations to levels that policymakers would find unacceptable.

These communication challenges might be particularly formidable in the case of adopting an intermediate target, such as nominal income. The public would be unfamiliar with this approach, and so might find it particularly hard to understand fully. Moreover, to guard against potential losses in credibility, the Committee would have to consider how to deal with issues such as periodic revisions to the data without leaving private agents with the impression that the FOMC is trying to evade its commitments. In principle, the Committee may also wish to consider "escape clauses" that adjust target variables for the effects of certain events, such as increases in indirect taxes and/or commodity prices. But, even if these contingencies are specified in advance, they might be perceived to being as opportunistically invoked as they occur. Moreover, too many escape clauses could weaken public confidence in the commitment to the target, and henceforth, limit the necessary building up of reputation that this policy requires over time.

A more general caveat is that the policy analysis we carry out in this paper is always conditional on the model used and, as we noted previously, on the baseline. No model contains the myriad of channels through which a major change in strategy might affect the economy. For example, the financial system could evolve endogenously in response to changes in monetary policy, expectations may adjust differently than we have assumed, and agents may have become more resistant to bearing risk than models, based as they are on the historical experience, suggest. Overall, the benefits of temporary increases in inflation in terms of additional stimulus to aggregate demand will be lower than expected if a sufficiently large fraction of agents are unable to respond to changes in the expected future real interest rates while other consumers, who merely consume their wage income, have their purchasing power eroded by the effect of unexpected price inflation on real wages. Finally, the primacy of expectations formation must be emphasized. The effects of the new policies could differ substantially if increases in inflation put upward pressure on term premiums that counteract, in part or in full, the intended stimulus, as we showed in figure 10.

Given these challenges and uncertainties, it is hard to be confident of the outcome of a change in the central bank's objective. That is not to say that the outcome will necessarily be adverse; one can imagine a range of possible outcomes depending on how the change is interpreted by the public. What our scenarios do effectively highlight, however, is how critical expectations formation is for the efficacy of policy at the effective lower bound. No central bank has successfully shifted from inflation targeting to nominal income targeting or used an increase in the inflation target as a stimulus tool—although of course the Bank of Japan is in the midst of just such an attempt and there is some reason for optimism. Expecting the unexpected thus would seem to be in order, and policymakers may well conclude that the potential benefits of a change in objective are not sufficient to outweigh the potential risks and costs that could result.[47]

B. How to integrate monetary policy and financial stability frameworks?

---

[47] Indeed, when the FOMC discussed nominal income targeting at its November 2011 meeting, participants agreed that such a change was not advisable at that time because of the "significant challenges associated with the adoption of such frameworks" (FOMC, 2011b).

Traditionally, central banks have had both monetary stability and financial stability objectives. For example, the Federal Reserve was founded in large part to address the bank runs that had occurred over the previous half century, and which had proven costly and disruptive. In contrast, its monetary policy objectives emerged clearly only over time (Bernanke (2013c)). But, in the decades running up to the financial crisis, central banks focused most of their attention on macroeconomic stability, with financial stability playing a lesser role (Bernanke (2011)).

During this period, many policymakers believed that monetary policy decisions could generally be made independently from financial stability considerations. In order for monetary policymakers to employ monetary policy to address financial stability concerns, three conditions would need to be met (Kohn (2006)). First, policymakers would need to be able to identify a building financial imbalance. Second, policymakers would need to judge that tighter monetary policy could help to limit the imbalance. And third, the use of monetary policy to address the imbalance would need to yield improved outcomes in terms of the policymakers' objectives for employment and inflation.[48] For example, if, to address the building imbalances, monetary policy would need to be tight enough to risk a significant economic slowdown, then the costs of taking the action might outweigh the benefits (Greenspan (2002)). In the face of these seemingly high hurdles to *a priori* monetary policy action, it generally appeared that the better course of action was to consider using regulatory and supervisory tools to address any emerging concerns, and if a financial crisis did occur, use monetary policy tools *ex post* to buffer the real economy from the resulting financial repercussions.

Following the crisis and the great recession, however, policymakers have reconsidered how to address possible threats to financial stability. In part, this reconsideration has been reflected in greatly increased efforts – exemplified in the United States by the passage of the Dodd-Frank Act – to ensure that the supervisory and regulatory tools are sufficient to address emerging imbalances before they can put the stability of the financial sector at risk. However, another result has been a reconsideration of the possible use of monetary policy to address financial stability concerns. While a detailed analysis of the regulatory response to the crisis is beyond the scope of this paper, this section takes up some of the issues raised by the need to broaden monetary policy frameworks to include financial stability considerations.

While a great deal of theoretical and empirical work stands behind existing monetary policy frameworks, it is only recently that work has begun on how to incorporate financial stability issues into the monetary policy framework. That said, a few conclusions seem appropriate at this point. First, to the extent possible, policymakers should use regulatory and supervisory tools to limit systemic risks rather than employing monetary policy. Such an approach would be desirable so long as the "macroprudential" tools are sufficient to greatly limit the risks of financial crisis, thereby limiting the need for monetary policy to deviate from the path that would be taken to best address the traditional monetary policy objectives of stable prices and maximum employment (Woodford (2012a), Svensson (2011)).

While it may be the case that macroprudential policy tools will prove sufficient to address financial stability concerns in many cases, it seems likely that such tools will not always be sufficient. Thus, situations may well arise in which policymakers will want to consider using

---

[48] For example, in terms of the discounted sum of squared deviations of inflation from target and the unemployment rate from its longer-run normal level.

monetary policy to address financial stability risks. However, monetary policy is likely to be a blunt instrument in such cases, and policymakers should balance the costs, in terms of their macroeconomic objectives, of deviating from the path for monetary policy that would otherwise be appropriate against the benefits in terms of reducing the probability or the costs of a possible future financial problem (Bernanke (2011), Woodford (2011)). It is important to note that such deviations could be in the direction either of more or less accommodative monetary policy (Bernanke (2013d)). In some cases, tighter policy may help to limit risk taking and accumulations of leverage, and so reduce the odds of a crisis (as assumed in Woodford (2012a), and discussed in Borio and Drehmann (2009)). Moreover, if low interest rates are leading financial market participants to take on excessive risk, then tighter monetary policy may "get in all the cracks" (Stein (2013)). As a result, it might help to limit risk taking by firms and investors that are not subject to prudential regulation or by entities that are not specifically identified by policymakers as taking on excessive risk. However, in other cases, tighter policy could, by undermining economic growth, lead to higher credit losses that would in turn weaken financial firms and undermine financial stability. And higher interest rates may in some cases increase the pace at which imbalances build, suggesting that lower interest rates could contribute to financial stability (Galí (2013)).[49]

In the near term, policymakers will need to make judgments about the use of monetary policy to address financial stability concerns without a complete framework for their decisions. Nonetheless, in order to better assess the appropriate stance of policy, central bankers will need to carefully monitor financial developments in order to anticipate possible financial stability risks. Indeed, the Federal Reserve has greatly increased its monitoring efforts in this area, both to inform its monetary policymaking and its supervisory activities, both independently and through the work of the Financial Stability Oversight Council. The monitoring focuses on emerging vulnerabilities, such as excessive leverage or maturity transformation, interconnectedness of firms and markets, and high levels of complexity. All of these features can potentially propagate and magnify financial shocks from a range of sources, and so undermine financial stability. This monitoring covers a wide range of financial markets and institutions, including systemically important financial institutions, the shadow banking sector, and key asset markets. The Federal Reserve's monitoring also encompasses the nonfinancial business sector and the household sector, since high levels of leverage in those sectors could lead to financial fragility in the face of shocks to the economy or asset prices.[50]

The Federal Reserve can use the information from its monitoring to take a range of steps to strengthen the financial sector and limit the risks to financial stability. Such steps, by heading off emerging vulnerabilities, can help policymakers to avoid the difficult decisions that may be required in a crisis. Most simply, the Federal Reserve can provide information through speeches and other communications regarding possible emerging risks to financial stability.[51] Such communications may lead private investors to reassess the risks associated with the specific instruments or transactions mentioned and thus, help to avoid a further buildup of risks.

---

[49] For additional discussion and a survey of the literature on the possible effects of monetary policy on financial stability, see IMF (2013).

[50] For additional information on the Federal Reserve's monitoring efforts, see Bernanke (2013b) and Adrian, Covitz, and Liang (2013).

[51] For example, see Stein (2013) discusses possible signs of "reaching for yield" in corporate credit markets, by agency REITs, and by commercial banks.

Alternatively, the Federal Reserve can use its traditional supervisory tools to address identified risks, for example by requiring specific institutions to take steps to strengthen their measurement and management of particular risks. Such supervisory decisions could be codified in formal agreements with the affected firms, in cease and desist orders, or in supervisory and regulatory (or SR) letters that ensure application of the approach to all entities supervised by the Federal Reserve.[52]

Of course, the Federal Reserve may not have the appropriate authority to address a potential risk to financial stability. In such cases, the Federal Reserve works with other supervisors through the Financial Stability Oversight Council (FSOC) to take the necessary steps to address the risk. For example, the FSOC has identified money market mutual funds as a potential financial stability risk, and has encouraged the Securities and Exchange Commission's ongoing efforts to address that risk (FSOC (2012)). And in the event that no supervisory agency has the necessary authority to address an emerging risk to financial stability, the FSOC can provide such authority by designating firms or activities as systemically important and providing for their oversight, or it can make recommendations to the Congress.

The Federal Reserve has also taken steps to make the banking system more resilient to shocks. Important efforts in this area include the tightening of capital and liquidity requirements under Basel III; the Federal Reserve recently completed major rulemakings on capital regulation (Federal Reserve (2013b)). These rules require larger amounts of higher-quality capital as well as impose a capital-conservation buffer that will ensure that banking organizations increase their capital when the economy performs well so that they will have the capital needed to sustain their lending in times of economic weakness. The new rules also impose a supplementary leverage ratio and a countercyclical capital buffer on the largest institutions, consistent with their systemic importance.[53]

An important new tool in assessing the appropriate level of capital for the largest banking institutions is the regular use of coordinated stress tests. Since the Supervisory Capital Assessment Program led by the Federal Reserve in 2009, the Federal Reserve has conducted systematic stress tests of the largest banking institutions in the United states on an annual basis. Moreover, starting this year, the Dodd-Frank Act requires additional stress testing of large banks.[54] These stress tests offer a number of benefits over more-traditional capital regulation.[55] First, by definition, they help ensure that the banking system can handle adverse tail events – that is, that the tested banks have enough capital to continue serving their customers even in the event of a highly adverse scenario. Second, the stress tests look horizontally across all of the largest banks rather than focusing on one specific bank at a time. This approach yields more consistent results and also provides macroprudential information on how the particular shocks considered would affect the largest banks as a whole. Finally, the public disclosure of stress test results provides investors with consistent information on the capital and financial condition of the largest banking organizations.

---

[52] We leave aside here the possible development of additional macroprudential tools. For a discussion of the interaction between monetary policy and a broader set of macroprudential policies, see IMF (2012).

[53] For a discussion, see Tarullo (2013).

[54] For a summary of results of the most recent Comprehensive Capital Analysis and Review, completed earlier this year, see Federal Reserve (2013a).

[55] For further discussion, see Bernanke (2013a).

The Federal Reserve has applied the information from its financial stability monitoring to its monetary policy decision-making process. Information on financial stability has been reported to the Federal Open Market Committee on a regular basis, and the Committee has discussed the information in the context of its policy decisions. Indeed, as noted earlier, the FOMC statement has explicitly conditioned the size, pace, and composition of asset purchases under the current purchase program on its assessment of the efficacy and costs of the purchases, and some Committee participants have noted specifically that an important possible cost of the program is its effects on financial stability.[56] Of course, balancing the benefits of additional purchases against these possible costs may not be straightforward, since it involves an assessment of the effects of changes in monetary policy on the odds of a financial crisis as well its possible costs, and a weighing of those potential costs against the expected benefits in terms of the Federal Reserve's employment and inflation goals (Kocherlakota (2013)). Moreover, those costs will depend on the economic situation, with tighter policy more costly when unemployment is higher and inflation lower than would be consistent with the Federal Reserve's mandate. As a result, all else equal, using monetary policy to combat financial stability risks may be more likely in a period of strong growth and developing financial imbalances than in a recovery.

Finally, a relevant question is what is the appropriate governance structure for policies related to financial stability? Since financial stability and monetary policy decisions are bound to be interrelated, there are clear benefits to having them made by the same policymakers. On the other hand, for reasons of accountability and clarity, there may be benefits to some separation. In particular, Fischer (2013), argues that financial stability policy is more likely to involve a draw on the fiscal authorities, and so should appropriately include a larger role for government, and a correspondingly reduced level of independence, compared with monetary policy decisions. Some have also argued that there may be reputational spillovers from financial supervision to monetary policymaking, which could make a separation of the two responsibilities important (Goodhart and Schoenmaker, 1995).[57]

Of course, no one-size-fits all institutional arrangement is likely to be appropriate in all cases since countries differ in their financial markets, political structures, and regulatory objectives, and also because they are starting from different historical backgrounds (Dixit, 1996). But that being said, there has been a clear shift in the direction of an increased role for central banks in financial stability. In the United States, as we have emphasized, financial stability has moved back to the forefront of policy discussions, and the Dodd-Frank Act has provided the Federal Reserve, as well as other supervisors, with additional tools to address financial stability concerns. The Bank of Japan has also increased its focus on financial stability even as it has taken steps to combat deflation. In the euro area, the ECB has been given responsibility for the direct supervision of the largest banks as part of the "Single Supervisory Mechanism" (ECB (2013b)). Most notably, in the United Kingdom, bank supervision has returned to the Bank of England in the form of the Prudential Regulation Authority, and the Bank's Financial Policy Committee has been given responsibility for identifying, monitoring, and taking action to remove or reduce systemic risk in the U.K. financial system (Bank of England (2013)). As these and other

---

[56] See, for example, Stein (2013).

[57] More recently, Goodhart as suggested that the rate-setting role of the central bank could be moved to another entity while the financial stability and lender-of-last-resort functions are retained by the central bank (Goodhart, 2010).

structures are tested over time, evidence will accumulate on the appropriate institutional structure for monetary and financial stability policy.

III. Concluding Remarks

In some ways, the changes to Federal Reserve's policy framework in recent years have moved the Federal Reserve considerably closer to inflation targeting. In particular, the Federal Reserve has now articulated a specific numerical inflation objective, and it has greatly increased its transparency regarding its assessment of the economic outlook and its policy plans through its post-meeting statements, the SEP, and press conferences. That being said, the approach taken by the Federal Reserve differs in important ways from a strict inflation targeting regime. Most obviously, the Federal Reserve has, by statute, a dual mandate. Of course, inflation targeting central banks generally employ "flexible inflation targeting" that takes account of the consequences of their actions for the real economy as well as inflation. Nonetheless, their formal accountability and much of their communications are in terms of inflation performance, and that is not the case for the Federal Reserve. Indeed, as noted earlier, the FOMC has clearly expressed it objectives for both employment and inflation and described its balanced approach for attaining those objectives in its Statement on Longer-Run Goals and Monetary Policy Strategy. A second difference, at least with respect to some inflation targeting central banks is that the Federal Reserve has considerable flexibility regarding the horizon over which it aims to return inflation to its longer-run goal. Again, as expressed in the Statement on Longer-Run Goals and Monetary Policy Strategy, the Committee will take account of the deviations from both of its goals when considering the appropriate policy stance. If, for example, employment is far below the level consistent with the dual mandate while inflation is above 2 percent, the Committee can take account of the large employment gap and aim to move inflation back to 2 percent more slowly than would otherwise be the case (Bernanke (2012b)). Finally, the dual mandate has played a significant role in the communication of the Committee's policy intentions. Thus, for example, the Committee has provided both unemployment rate and inflation rate thresholds in its forward guidance for the federal funds rate. An inflation targeting central bank might instead put such forward guidance in terms of the inflation rate only.[58]

While the Federal Reserve and other major central banks have made significant changes to their monetary policy frameworks in recent years, it is to be expected that these frameworks will continue to evolve. Research and experience will yield improvements in frameworks for monetary policy and financial stability policy as well as suggesting new ways to better integrate the two. Moreover, new economic developments and challenges may call for new tools and changes in communications to make those tools more effective. While they cannot anticipate how these changes will play out, central banks should remain flexible over time to ensure that

---

[58] For example, the Bank of Canada's conditional policy guidance in April 2009 indicated that, "Conditional on the outlook for inflation, the target overnight rate can be expected to remain at its current level until the end of the second quarter of 2010 in order to achieve the inflation target." (See http://www.bankofcanada.ca/2009/04/publications/press-releases/fad-press-release-2009-04-21/). That being said, as discussed above, the recent forward guidance provided by the Bank of England included references to both unemployment and inflation.

their frameworks are changed appropriately in order to best support the success of their economies.

Table 1. Recent Innovations in Federal Reserve Communications Regarding Monetary Policy Goals and Strategy

Date	Innovation	Purpose
December 2005	Timing of the release of the minutes shortened to three weeks	Provide more timely information on the range of participants' views
November 2007	Summary of Economic Projections (SEP)	To provide information on the Committee's outlook for the economy
January 2009	Addition of longer-run projections to the SEP	To provide information on the Committee's longer-run goals
April 2011	Post-meeting press conferences	To provide more comprehensive and timely information on the decision and views of the Committee
January 2012	Addition of federal funds rate to the SEP	To provide information on the Committee's policy expectations
January 2012	Statement on Longer-run Goals and Policy Strategy	To provide information on the Committee's assessment of the rate of inflation consistent with its dual mandate and the longer-run normal unemployment rate

Table 2.   Influence of threshold settings and the post-firming policy rule on the expected timing of threshold crossing and related factors, derived from stochastic simulations of a small FRB/US model

	[1]	[2]	[3]	[4]	[5]	[6]	[7]
	Median Date of First Time		Percentage of Crossings Caused by Reaching the:		Policy Maker Loss		Welfare
	Crossing	Firming	Unemployment Threshold	Inflation Threshold	Mean	Median	Improvement Share
Inertial Taylor Rule							
u = 5.0; π = 2.5	2015:Q3	2015:Q4	59.62	42.99	97.92	78.2	81.42
u = 5.5; π = 2.5	2015:Q3	2015:Q4	66.49	36.33	102.38	82.7	85.08
u = 6.0; π = 2.5	2015:Q2	2015:Q4	73.24	29.69	105.85	85.71	87.92
u = 6.5; π = 1.5	2014:Q2	2014:Q4	50.88	53.5	111.3	92.09	94.71
u = 6.5; π = 2.0	2014:Q4	2015:Q2	68.7	34.72	109.17	89.91	92.84
u = 6.5; π = 2.5	2014:Q4	2015:Q3	79.69	22.88	108.45	89.21	91.26
u = 6.5; π = 2.5	2014:Q2	2015:Q1	86.67	15.44	110.5	91.31	94.05

Table 3. Summary of Unconventional Monetary Policies in the Major Foreign Central Banks

Bank of Japan

Program/Facility	Size of program	Description
Asset Purchase Program (APP) (June 2010 to December 2012)	Initially set at ¥35 trillion (7 percent of GDP), gradually increased to ¥101 trillion (21 percent of GDP).	The APP was part of a Comprehensive Monetary Easing program aimed at reducing term and risk premia. The APP covered government securities, corporate bonds, commercial paper, exchange-traded funds, and real estate investment trusts. Asset purchases were complemented by a commitment to maintaining zero interest rates until the BOJ judged that price stability was in sight on the basis of its "medium- to long-term understanding of price stability (i.e. 1 percent)." Purchases were unsterilized and maturing assets were not reinvested.
Quantitative and Qualitative Monetary Easing (April 2013 to present)	Monetary base will increase at an annual pace of about 60-70 trillion yen (13–15 percent of GDP).	This program replaced the CME. It sets an explicit two-year time horizon to achieve a 2 percent inflation target. JGB purchases were increased to ¥50 trillion a year (from ¥20 trillion), the average maturity of JGBs purchased was extended to 7 years (from 3 years or less), the size of ETF purchases was doubled to ¥1 trillion, and the size of J-REIT purchases was tripled to ¥30 billion a year. Purchases were unsterilized and maturing assets were not reinvested.
Loan Support Program (June 2010 to March 2018)	¥5.5 trillion (1¼ percent of GDP)	The Loan support program is a series of initiative to support private financial institutions' efforts in strengthening the foundations for economic growth. Under the largest initiative, the "Growth-Supporting Funding Facility," the BOJ provides loans to financial institutions for up to four years at favorable terms provided these funds are then used to finance investments in pre-determined growth-enhancing activities, such as medicine and nursing care, environment and energy, agriculture, tourism, and forestry and fisheries.

Table 3. Summary of Unconventional Monetary Policies in the Major Foreign Central Banks (continued)

European Central Bank

Program/Facility	Size of program	Description
Outright asset purchase programs (various programs, sterilized, starting July 2009)	SMP: €208.7 billion (2¼ percent of GDP); OMT: unlimited, not yet activated; Covered Bond Purchase Programs: €76 billion (¾ percent of GDP) in total purchases.	Securities Market Programme: The ECB bought €208.7 billion in peripheral euro-area public and private debt securities. The program was in operation from May 2010 to August 2012. Outright Monetary Transactions: The program was launched in August 2012 and allows the ECB to purchase short-term sovereign debt of euro-area countries that are subject to an appropriate European Financial Stability Facility/European Stability Mechanism macroeconomic adjustment program. Covered Bond Purchase Programmes: The ECB purchased €60 billion in covered bonds from July 2009 to June 2010 under its first program and €16 billion out of a maximum of €40 billion from November 2011 to October 2012 under its second program.
Long–Term Refinancing Operations	About 11 percent of GDP.	Between late 2009 and early 2012, the ECB conducted a series of unsterilized one-year and three-year long-term refinancing operations (LTROs) on a full allotment basis. Its three-year LTROs in December 2011 and February 2012 allotted €489 billion (5¼ percent of GDP) and €530 billion (5½ percent of GDP), respectively.
Guidance on future policy rates (starting July 2013)	n.a.	On July 4, 2013, the ECB Governing Council added the following language to the introductory statement from the ECB president's press conference: "The Governing Council expects the key ECB interest rates to remain at present or lower levels for an extended period of time. This expectation is based on the overall subdued outlook for inflation extending into the medium term, given the broad-based weakness in the real economy and subdued monetary dynamics."

41

Table 3. Summary of Unconventional Monetary Policies in the Major Foreign Central Banks (continued)

Bank of England

Program/Facility	Size of program	Description
Asset Purchase Facility (APF) (March 2009 to present)	£375 billion (24 percent of U.K. GDP).	The APF implements the BOE quantitative easing program. Over 99 percent of assets are gilts, with corporate bonds and asset-back securities accounting for the residual. The U.K. Treasury fully indemnifies the BOE in the advent of APF losses. Maturing assets are reinvested to maintain the size of the program.
Funding for Lending Scheme (FLS) (Borrowing period: August 2012 to January 2015. Rollover period: four years from drawdown date.)	£80 billion (5 percent of U.K. GDP) if all banks participate and maintain existing lending, unlimited if lending increases. As of March 31, 2013, £16.5 billion in bank assets had been swapped.	The FLS is designed to incentivize banks and building societies to boost their lending to the U.K. real economy. It provides funding to banks and building societies for an extended period, with both the price and quantity of funding provided linked to their lending performance. From August 1, 2012 to January 31, 2014, participating banks are able to swap a wide range of assets for 9-month U.K. Treasury Bills, subject to fees and haircuts.
Forward guidance (August 7, 2013 to present)	n.a.	The guidance is formulated as follows: "The [Monetary Policy Committee] intends not to raise Bank Rate from its current level of 0.5% at least until the Labour Force Survey headline measure of the unemployment rate has fallen to a threshold of 7%, subject to the conditions below. [...] But until the unemployment threshold is reached, and subject to the conditions below, the MPC intends not to reduce the stock of asset purchases financed by the issuance of central bank reserves and, consistent with that, intends to reinvest the cash flows associated with all maturing gilts held in the Asset Purchase Facility. The guidance [...] would cease to hold if any of the following three 'knockouts' were breached: • in the MPC's view, it is more likely than not, that CPI inflation 18 to 24 months ahead will be 0.5 percentage points or more above the 2% target; • medium-term inflation expectations no longer remain sufficiently well anchored; • the Financial Policy Committee (FPC) judges that the stance of monetary policy poses a significant threat to financial stability that cannot be contained by the substantial range of mitigating policy actions available to the FPC, the Financial Conduct Authority and the Prudential Regulation Authority in a way consistent with their objectives."

42

Appendix A: The "small FRB/US" model

The model employed in this paper is a small-scale version of the Board staff's FRB/US model. As documented in a sequence of papers,[59] FRB/US can be described as an elaborate, large-scale version of a New Keynesian model. The larger model contains structures designed to allow the model to consider a wide range of economic phenomena, consistent with its role as the central domestic economy model at the Board. However, for the class of experiments of interest in this paper—experiments that center on the monetary transmission mechanism in general and expectations formation in particular—a much simpler model can capture the essence of FRB/US.

As in the original model, agents in what we might call "small FRB/US" formulate decision rules by choosing a target path for the decision variable of interest, subject to an adjustment cost function. Small FRB/US condenses the decisions of a variety of agents into a single decision maker who can be thought of as choosing a target path for consumption, to minimize an adjustment cost function. The order of adjustment costs could be as high as three; however, the key behavioral equations of FRB/US and hence, of small FRB/US, involve second-order adjustment costs, which means that it is costly to adjust the growth rate of the decision variable. For a generic variable, x_t the cost function is as follows:

$$L = \min \sum_{i=0}^{\infty} \beta^i \left\{ \left(x_t - x_t^*\right)^2 + b_1 (\Delta x_{t+i})^2 + b_2 (\Delta x_{t+i} - \Delta x_{t+i}^*)^2 \right\} \qquad (A.1)$$

where β is the discount factor and b_1, b_2 are adjustment cost parameters. Equation (A1) can be thought of as a generalization of the standard quadratic level-adjustment cost functions popularized, for example, by Rotemberg (1982) in the case of price-setting agents. The solution to the above problem results in a decision rule, which can be written in extended error-correction form:

$$\Delta x_t = \lambda_1 \left(x_{t-1}^* - x_{t-1}\right) + \lambda_2 \Delta x_{t-1} + z_t + \varepsilon_t \qquad (A.2)$$

where z_t is the weighted sum of expected future changes in the target variable along the desired path toward steady-state equilibrium, which, in this second-order adjustment-cost case is:

$$z_t = \lambda_1 \Delta x_t^* - \lambda_1 \lambda_2 \beta^2 \Delta x_{t+1}^* + \left(1 - \lambda_1 + \lambda_2\right) \beta E_t z_{t+1} - \lambda_2 \beta^2 E_t z_{t+2}. \qquad (A.3)$$

For "small FRB/US," we can think of the two decision variables covered by this formulation as consumption and the consumption price level; monetary policy is taken as being governed by any of the several Taylor-type rules described in Appendix C, or by an optimal control policy.

The target paths—that is, the z-variables—that enter the dynamic adjustment equations are as follows:

$$gap_t^* = \lambda_3 (rrl_t^* - rrl_t^\infty) + \lambda_4 zgap_t + (1 - \lambda_4) gap_t \qquad (A.4)$$

---

[59] See, e.g., Brayton and Tinsley (1996).

$$rrl_t^* = \lambda_5 rrl_{t+1} + (1 - \lambda_5)(R_t - \pi_t + \lambda_6 gap_t) \qquad (A.5)$$

$$zgap_t^* = \lambda_7 zgap_{t+1} + (1 - \lambda_7) gap_t. \qquad (A.6)$$

Equation (A.4) gives that the desired output gap, conditional on adjustment costs, is a function of the deviation of the target level of the long-term real interest rate, rrl_t, from its equilibrium level, and a weighted average of the current output gap and a geometric sum of future output gaps. The latter is specified in equation (A.6). Equation (A.5) shows that the target level of the long-term real interest rate is a geometric sum of short-term real interest rates plus an output gap term; the latter captures the relationship between term premiums and the state of the economy.

Appendix B: The baseline

As noted in the main text, the quantitative results described in this paper will exhibit some sensitivity to the particular features of the baseline owing, among other things, to the implications of the effective lower bound. Accordingly, in this brief appendix, we describe in words the central features of the baseline. It should be noted that the qualitative results will not differ substantially for alternative baselines that are in the neighborhood of one described here.

The construction of the baseline begins with the National Income and Product Accounts for 2013:Q2, as they were seen in July 2013, together with a characterization of the state of resource utilization that is consistent with those accounts. All of the scenarios described in this paper begin in 2013:Q3. In our baseline, we assume that the output gap is −2.8 percent as of that date, and the unemployment rate is 7.5 percent, which with a natural rate of unemployment of 5½ percent corresponds to an unemployment gap of 2 percentage points. The output gap is assumed to close slowly over time, reaching zero at the end of 2018; the labor market gap closes at about the same date. Inflation as measured by the four-quarter rate of change in core PCE prices is 1.1 percent in 2013:Q3 and climbs slowly to reach the target rate of inflation of 2 percent in 2020. The path for the federal funds rate that supports this outlook remains at the effective lower bound until the first quarter of 2016 after which it climbs moderately quickly, reaching 4 percent in 2021.

Appendix C: The simple monetary policy rules

The table below gives the expressions for the policy rules used in this paper. In the table, R_t denotes the nominal federal funds rate for quarter t, while the right-hand-side variables include the model's projection of trailing four-quarter core PCE inflation for the current quarter and three quarters ahead (π_t and $\pi_{t+3|t}$), the output gap estimate for the current period as well as its one-quarter-ahead forecast (gap_t and $gap_{t+1|t}$), and the forecast of the three-quarter-ahead annual change in the output gap ($\Delta^4 gap_{t+3|t}$). The value of policymakers' long-run inflation objective, denoted π^*, is 2 percent. The nominal income targeting rule responds to the nominal income gap four quarters ahead, which is defined as the difference between nominal income yn_t (100 times the log of the level of nominal GDP) and a target value yn_t^* (100 times the log of target nominal GDP). Target nominal GDP in 2007:Q4 is set equal to actual nominal GDP in that quarter and then projected forward at a rate of 2 percentage points per year faster than conventional estimates of potential GDP, about 2½ percent per year.

Taylor (1993) rule	$R_t = rr^* + \pi_t + 0.5(\pi_t - \pi^*) + 0.5gap_t$
Taylor (1999) rule	$R_t = rr^* + \pi_t + 0.5(\pi_t - \pi^*) + gap_t$
Inertial Taylor (1999) rule	$R_t = 0.85R_{t-1} + 0.15(rr^* + \pi_t + 0.5(\pi_t - \pi^*) + gap_t)$
First-difference rule	$R_t = R_{t-1} + 0.5(\pi_{t+3|t} - \pi^*) + 0.5\Delta^4 gap_{t+3|t}$
Nominal income targeting rule	$R_t = 0.75R_{t-1} + 0.25(rr^* + \pi_t + yn_{t+4|t} - yn^*_{t+4})$

The first two of the selected rules were studied by Taylor (1993, 1999). The inertial Taylor (1999) rule is a straightforward extension of the Taylor (1999) rule. The long-run real interest rates appearing in the Taylor (1993, 1999) rules and the inertial Taylor (1999) rule are set a bit over 2 percent. A feature of the first-difference rule is that its prescriptions do not depend on the level of the output gap or the long-run real interest rate (see Orphanides, 2003).

References

Adam, Klaus and Roberto M. Billi (2007). "Discretionary Monetary Policy and the Zero Lower Bound on Nominal Interest Rates," *Journal of Monetary Economics*, vol. 54, no. 3, 728-752.

Adrian, Tobias, Daniel Covitz, and Nellie Liang (2013). "Financial Stability Monitoring," *Finance and Economics Discussion Series*, no. 2013-21.

Ascari, Guido and Argia Sbordone (2013). "The Macroeconomics of Trend Inflation," *Staff Report*, no. 628, Federal Reserve Bank of New York, New York.

Bank of England (2013). "Annual Report 2013."

Bank of Japan (2006). "The Bank's Thinking on Price Stability," March 10.

Bank of Japan (2012). "The Price Stability Goal in the Medium to Long Term," February 14.

Bank of Japan (2013a). "The 'Price Stability Target' under the Framework for the Conduct of Monetary Policy," January 22.

Bank of Japan (2013b). "Introduction of the 'Quantitative and Qualitative Monetary Easing,'" April 4.

Bauer, Michael D. and Glenn D. Rudebusch (2011). "The Signaling Channel for Federal Reserve Bond Purchases," Federal Reserve Bank of San Francisco, *Working Paper Series*, no. 2011-21.

Bernanke, Ben S. (2004). "Inflation Targeting," Remarks at Federal Reserve Bank of St. Louis, St. Louis, Missouri.

Bernanke, Ben S. (2007). "Central Banking and Bank Supervision in the United States," Remarks at the American Economic Association Annual Meetings.

Bernanke, Ben S. (2011). "The Effects of the Great Recession on Central Bank Doctrine and Practice," Remarks at the Federal Reserve Bank of Boston 56th Economic Conference, Boston, Massachusetts.

Bernanke, Ben S. (2012a). Testimony before the Senate Banking Committee (Q&A session), February 7.

Bernanke, Ben S. (2012b). "Monetary Policy since the Onset of the Crisis," Remarks at the Federal Reserve Bank of Kansas City Economic Symposium, Jackson Hole, Wyoming, August 31.

Bernanke, Ben S. (2013a). "Stress Testing Banks: What Have We Learned?" Remarks at the Financial Markets Conference, *Maintaining Financial Stability: Holding a Tiger by the Tail*, sponsored by the Federal Reserve Bank of Atlanta, Stone Mountain, Georgia, April 8.

Bernanke, Ben S. (2013b). "Monitoring the Financial System," Remarks at the 49th Annual Conference on Bank Structure and Competition sponsored by the Federal Reserve Bank of Chicago, Chicago, Illinois, May 10.

Bernanke, Ben S. (2013c). "A Century of U.S. Central Banking: Goals, Frameworks, Accountability," Remarks at the conference, *The First 100 Years of the Federal Reserve: The Policy Record, Lessons Learned, and Prospects for the Future*, sponsored by the National Bureau of Economic Research, Cambridge, Massachusetts, July 10.

Bernanke, Ben S. (2013d). "Long-Term Interest Rates," Remarks at the Annual Monetary/Macroeconomics Conference: The Past and Future of Monetary Policy, sponsored by Federal Reserve Bank of San Francisco, San Francisco, California.

Blanchard, Olivier, Giovanni Dell'Ariccia, and Paolo Mauro (2010). "Rethinking Macroeconomic Policy," *IMF Staff Positional Note*, International Monetary Fund, Washington, D.C., February.

Borio, Claudio and Mathias Drehmann (2009). "Assessing the Risk of Banking Crises – Revisited," *Quarterly Review*, Bank for International Settlements, March 2.

Brainard, William C. (1967). "Uncertainty and the Effectiveness of Policy," *American Economic Review*, vol. 57, no. 2, pp. 411-425.

Brayton, Flint (2013). "FRB/US on Small Scale," mimeo, Federal Reserve Board, Washington, D.C., May.

Brayton, Flint and Peter Tinsley (Eds.) (1996). "A Guide to FRB/US: A Macroeconomic Model of the United States," *Finance and Economics Discussion Series*, Board of Governors of the Federal Reserve System, Washington, D.C.

Brunnermeier, Markus K. and Christian Julliard (2008). "Money Illusion and Housing Frenzies,"

Review of Financial Studies, vol. 21, no. 1, pp. 135-180.

Chung, Hess, Jean-Philippe Laforte, David Reifschneider, and John C. Williams (2012). "Have We Underestimated the Likelihood and Severity of Zero Lower Bound Events?" *Journal of Money, Credit and Banking*, vol. 44, pp. 47-82.

Coibion, Oliver, Yuri Gorodnichenko and Johannes. F. Wieland (2012). "The optimal inflation rate in New Keynesian models: Should central banks raise their inflation targets in light of the ZLB?," *The Review of Economic Studies,* 79, pp.1371—1406.

D'Amico, Stefania, William English, David López-Salido, and Edward Nelson (2012). "The Federal Reserve's Large-Scale Asset Purchase Programs: Rationale and Effects," *Economic Journal*, vol. 122, no. 564, pp. 415-46.

Dixit, Avinash (1996). *The Making of Economic Policy: A Transaction-Cost Politics Perspective*, MIT Press, Cambridge, Massachusetts.

Eggertsson, Gauti B. and Michael Woodford (2003). "The Zero Bound on Interest Rates and Optimal Monetary Policy," *Brookings Papers on Economic Activity*, vol. 34, pp. 139-211.

English, William B., William R. Nelson and Brian P. Sack (2003). "Interpreting the Significance of the Lagged Interest Rate in Estimated Monetary Policy Rules," *Contributions to Macroeconomics*, vol. 3, no. 1.

European Central Bank (2011). "The Monetary Policy of the ECB."

European Central Bank (2013a). "Introductory Statement to the Press Conference," August 1.

European Central Bank (2013b). "ECB welcomes European Parliament vote to create single supervisory mechanism," Press Release, September 12.

Evans, George and Seppo Honkapohja (2001). (Eds.) *Learning and Expectations in Macroeconomics* (with Seppo Honkapohja), Princeton University Press, January 2001.

Federal Open Market Committee (2005). Minutes of the January 2005 FOMC meeting.

Federal Open Market Committee (2009). FOMC Statement, March 18.

Federal Open Market Committee (2011a). FOMC Statement, August 9.

Federal Open Market Committee (2011b). Minutes from the FOMC meeting, November 1-2.

Federal Open Market Committee (2012). FOMC Statement, December 12.

Federal Reserve (2011). Press release, March 24.

Federal Reserve (2013a). Press release, March 14.

Federal Reserve (2013b). Press release, July 2.

Financial Stability Oversight Council (2012). "Proposed Recommendations Regarding Money Market Mutual Fund Reform," *Federal Register*, vol. 77, no. 223.

Fischer, Stanley (1981). "Towards an Understanding of the Costs of Inflation: II," *Carnegie-Rochester Conference Series on Public Policy*, vol. 15, no. 1, pp. 5-41.

Fischer, Stanley (2013). "Macroprudential Policy: Israel," Remarks at the *Rethinking Macro Policy II: First Steps and Early Lessons* conference, International Monetary Fund, April 16-17.

Fregert, Klas and Lars Jonung (1999). "Monetary Regimes and Endogenous Wage Contracts: Sweden 1908-1995," Stockholm School of Economics.

Gali, Jordi (2008). "The New Keynesian Approach to Monetary Policy Analysis: Lessons and New Directions," Universitat Pompeu Fabra Department of Economics and Business, *Economics Working Papers*, no. 1075.

Gali, Jordi (2013). "Monetary Policy and Rational Asset Prices Bubbles," *American Economic Review*, forthcoming.

Goodhart, Charles (2010). "The Changing Role of Central Banks" Bank for International Settlements, *Working Papers*, no. 326.

Goodhart, Charles and Dirk Schoenmaker (1995). "Should the Functions of Monetary Policy and Banking Supervision be Separated?" *Oxford Economic Papers*, vol. 47, no. 4, pp. 539-560.

Greenspan, Alan (1988). Statement before the Committee on Banking, Finance, and Urban Affairs, U.S. Senate, July 13.

Greenspan, Alan (2002). "Economic volatility," Remarks at a symposium sponsored by the Federal Reserve Bank of Kansas City, Jackson Hole, Wyoming, August 30.

HM Treasury (2003). "The Remit to the Monetary Policy Committee," December 10.

HM Treasury (2013). "Remit for the Monetary Policy Committee," March 20.

International Monetary Fund (2012). "The Interaction of Monetary Policy and Macroprudential Policies – Background Paper," December 27.

International Monetary Fund (2013). "The Interaction of Monetary and Macroprudential Policies," January 29.

Kato, Ryo and Shin-Ichi Nishiyama (2005). "Optimal Monetary Policy when Interest Rates are Bounded at Zero," *Journal of Economic Dynamics and Control*, vol. 29, no. 1-2, pp. 97-133.

Kocherlakota, Naryana (2013). Remarks at the 61st Annual Management Conference of the University of Chicago Booth School of Business, Chicago, Illinois, May 17.

Kohn, Donald L. (2006). "Monetary policy and asset prices," Remarks at *Monetary Policy: A Journey from Theory to Practice*, a European Central Bank Colloquium held in honor of Otmar Issing, Frankfurt, Germany, March 16.

Kohn, Donald L. (2007). "John Taylor Rules," Remarks at the *Conference on John Taylor's Contributions to Monetary Theory and Policy*, Federal Reserve Bank of Dallas, Dallas, Texas, October 12, 2007.

Krishnamurthy, Arvind and Anette Vissing-Jorgensen (2011). "The Effects of Quantitative Easing on Long-term Interest Rates," *Brookings Papers on Economic Activity*, September 2011.

Krishnamurthy, Arvind and Annette Vissing-Jorgensen (2013). "The Ins and Outs of LSAPs," Presented at the Federal Reserve Bank of Kansas City's Jackson Hole Symposium on the *Global Dimensions of Unconventional Monetary Policy*, Jackson Hole, Wyoming, August.

Lindsey, David (2003). "A Modern History of FOMC Communication: 1975-2002," Board of Governors of the Federal Reserve System, Washington, D.C., June 24, 2003.

McCallum, Bennett T. and Edward Nelson (1999). "Nominal Income Targeting in an Open-Economy Optimizing Model," *Journal of Monetary Economics*, vol. 43, pp. 553–578.

McCallum, Bennett T. and Edward Nelson (2005). "Targeting vs. Instrument Rules for Monetary Policy," Federal Reserve Bank of St. Louis *Review*, September/October 2005, vol. 87, no. 5, pp. 597-611.

Meyer, Laurence (2000). "Structural Change and Monetary Policy," Remarks before the Joint Conference of the Federal Reserve Bank of San Francisco and the Stanford Institute for Economic Policy Research, Federal Reserve Bank of San Francisco, San Francisco, California, March 3.

Mishkin, Frederic S. (2007a). "Monetary Policy and the Dual Mandate," Remarks at Bridgewater College, Bridgewater, Virginia, April 10, 2007.

Mishkin, Frederic S. (2007b). "The Federal Reserve's Enhanced Communications Strategy and the Science of Monetary Policy," Remarks to the Undergraduate Economics Association, Massachusetts Institute of Technology, Cambridge, Massachusetts, November 29, 2007.

Orphanides, Athanasios (2003). "Historical Monetary Policy Analysis and the Taylor Rule," *Journal of Monetary Economics*, vol. 50, no. 5, pp. 983-1022.

Orphanides, Athanasios, and Volker Wieland (2000). "Efficient Monetary Policy Design Near Price Stability," *Journal of the Japanese and International Economies*, 14(4), pp. 327–365.

Reifschneider, David and John C. Williams (2000). "Three Lessons for Monetary Policy in a Low-Inflation Era," *Journal of Money, Credit, and Banking*, vol. 32, no. 4, pp. 936-966.

Rogers, John, Chiara Scotti, and Jonathan Wright (2013). "Evaluating Asset-Market Effects of Unconventional Monetary Policy: A Cross-Country Comparison," (manuscript in preparation).

Rotemberg, Julio J. (1982). "Sticky Prices in the United States," *Journal of Political Economy*, vol. 90, no. 6, pp. 1187-1211.

Rudebusch, Glenn D. (2006). "Monetary Policy Inertia: fact or fiction?" *International Journal of Central Banking*, vol. 2, no. 4, pp. 85-135.

Rudebusch, Glenn D., and Lars E.O. Svensson (1999). "Policy Rules for Inflation Targeting."

In J.B. Taylor (ed.), *Monetary Policy Rules*, Chicago: University of Chicago Press. 203–253.

Stein, Jeremy (2013). "Overheating in Credit Markets: origins, measurement, and policy responses," Speech given to the symposium on *Restoring Household Financial Stability After the Great Recession,* Federal Reserve Bank of St. Louis, St. Louis, Missouri, February 7.

Summers, Lawrence H. (1991). "Planning for the Next Financial Crisis," In Martin Feldstein (Eds.), *The Risk of Economic Crisis* (University of Chicago Press, 1991), pp. 135-158.

Svensson, Lars E.O. (2003). "What is Wrong with Taylor Rules? Using Judgment in Monetary Policy through Targeting Rules," *Journal of Economic Literature*, vol. 41, no. 2, pp. 426-477.

Svensson, Lars E.O. (2005). "Targeting versus Instrument Rules for Monetary Policy: What Is Wrong with McCallum and Nelson?" Federal Reserve Bank of St. Louis *Review*, September/October 2005, vol. 87, no. 5, pp. 613-625.

Svensson, Lars E.O, (2011). "Inflation Targeting," In Benjamin M. Friedman and Michael Woodford (Eds.), *Handbook of Monetary Economics* (North Holland, 2010), Chap. 22, pp. 1237-1302.

Svensson, Lars E.O, (2013). "Forward Guidance as a Monetary Policy Tool in Theory and Practice: The Swedish Experience," paper presented at the NBER Conference "Lessons from the Financial Crisis for Monetary Policy", Boston, October 18-19, 2013.

Tarullo, Daniel K. (2013). "Evaluating Progress in Regulatory Reforms to Promote Financial Stability," Speech given at the Peterson Institute for International Economics, Washington, D.C., May 3.

Taylor, John B. (1993). "Discretion versus Policy Rules in Practice," *Carnegie-Rochester Conference Series on Public Policy*, vol. 39, no. 1, pp. 195-214.

Taylor, John B. (1999a). "A Historical Analysis of Monetary Policy Rules," In John B. Taylor (Ed.), *Monetary Policy Rules* (University of Chicago Press, 1999), pp. 319-348.

Taylor, John B. (1999). *Monetary Policy Rules*, University of Chicago Press, 1999.

Taylor, John B. and John C. Williams (2011). "Simple and Robust Rules for Monetary Policy," In Benjamin M. Friedman and Michael Woodford (Eds.), *Handbook of Monetary Economics* (North Holland, 2010), Chap. 15, pp. 829-859.

Woodford, Michael (2003). *Interest and Prices: Foundations of a Theory of Monetary Policy,* Princeton University Press, Princeton, August 18, 2003.

Woodford, Michael (2011). "Optimal Monetary Stabilization Policy" In Benjamin M. Friedman and Michael Woodford (Eds.), *Handbook of Monetary Economics* (North Holland, 2010), Chap. 14, pp. 723-828.

Woodford, Michael (2012a). "Inflation Targeting and Financial Stability," National Bureau of Economic Research, *NBER Working Papers*, no. 17967.

Woodford, Michael (2012b). "Methods of Policy Accommodation at the Interest-rate Lower Bound," Paper presented at the Federal Reserve Bank of Kansas City Symposium on *The Changing Policy Landscape*, Jackson Hole, Wyoming, August 31.

Yellen, Janet L. (2012). "Revolution and Evolution in Central Bank Communications," Speech given at the University of California Haas School of Business, Berkeley, California November 13.

Figure 1
Performance of simple policy rules
(Baseline conditions)

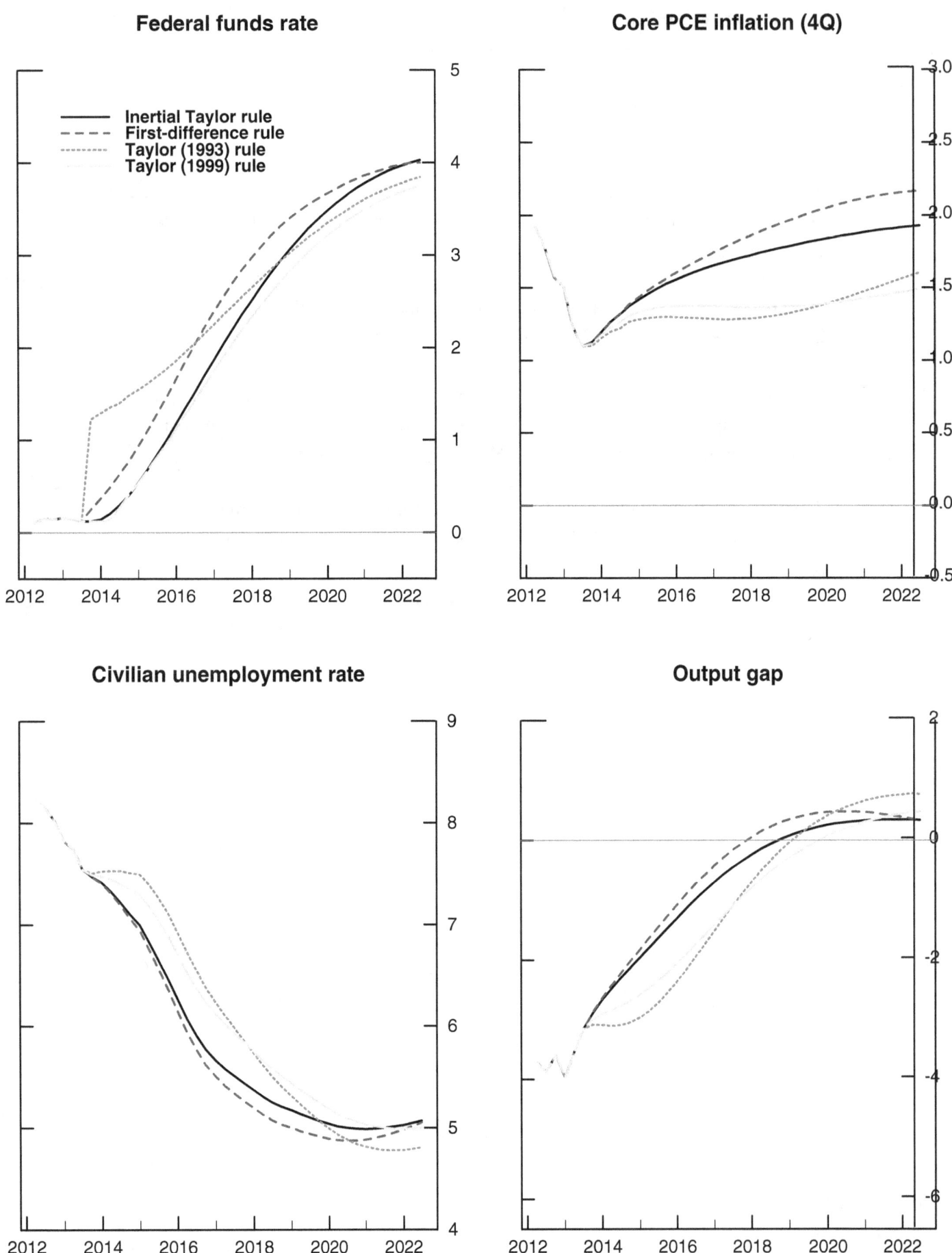

Federal funds rate

- Inertial Taylor rule
- First-difference rule
- Taylor (1993) rule
- Taylor (1999) rule

Core PCE inflation (4Q)

Civilian unemployment rate

Output gap

Figure 2
Probability of liftoff from the effective lower bound by calendar date
(Stochastic simulations under simple policy rules, baseline conditions)

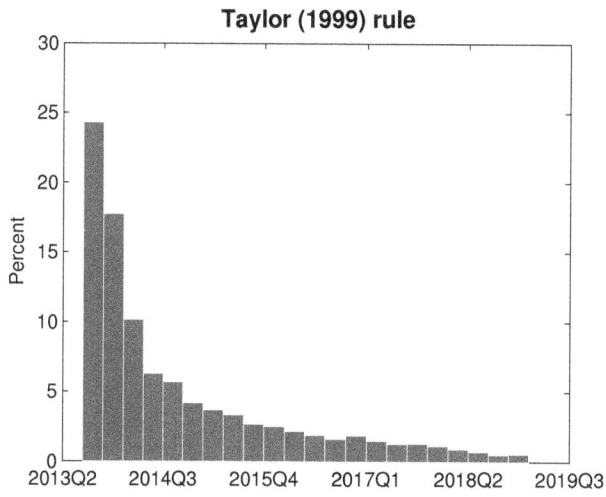

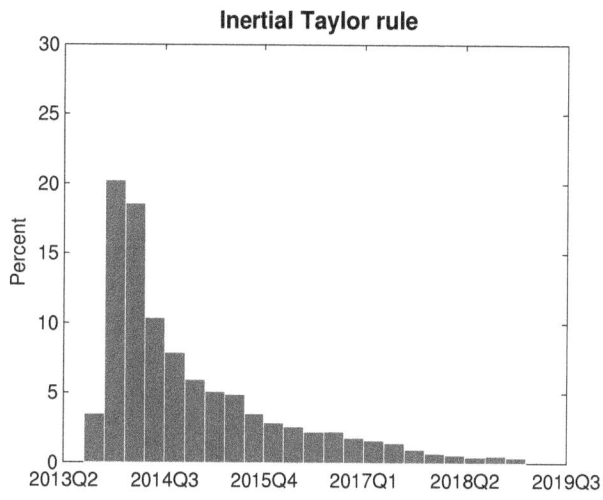

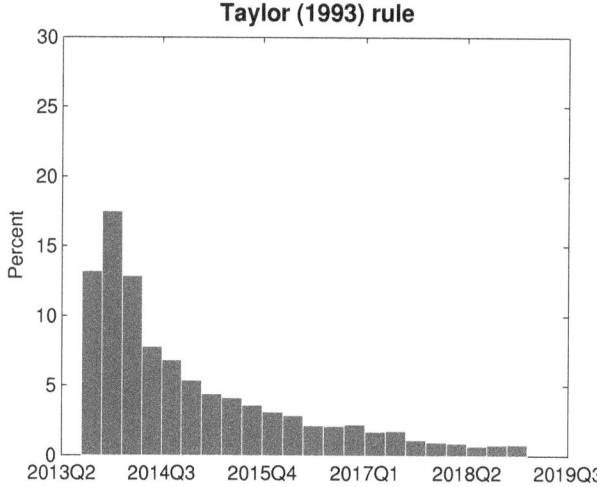

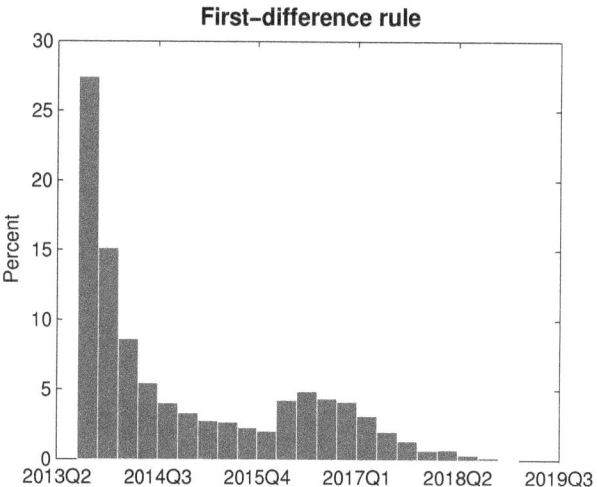

Figure 3
Probability of returning to the effective lower bound within four quarters of first liftoff
(Stochastic simulations under simple policy rules, baseline conditions)

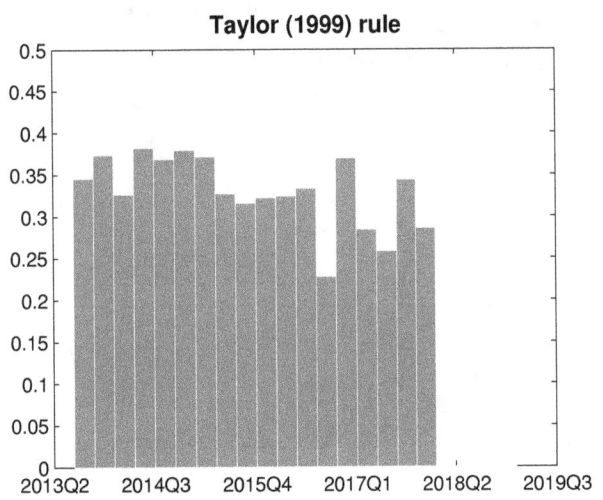

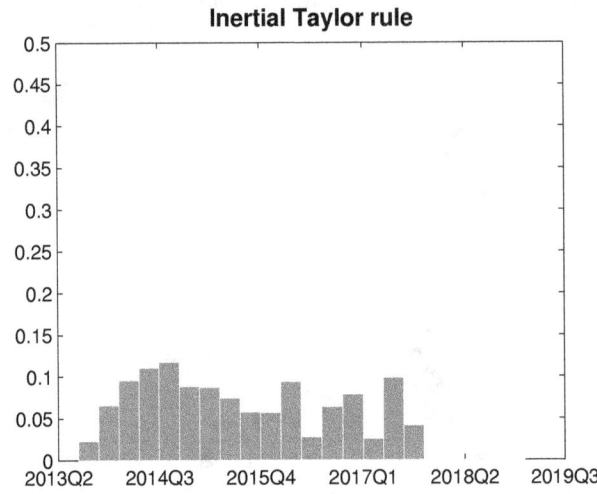

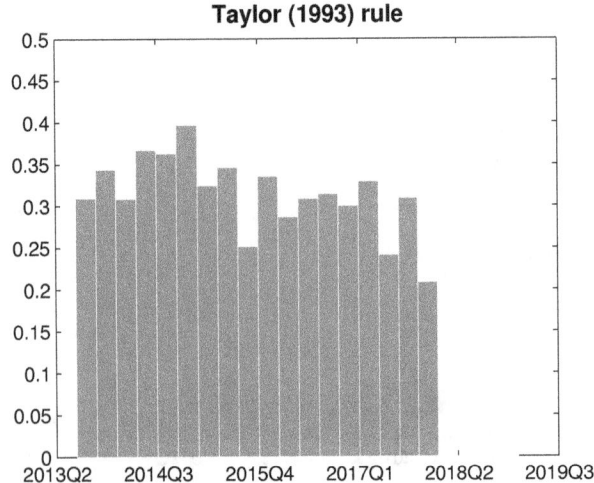

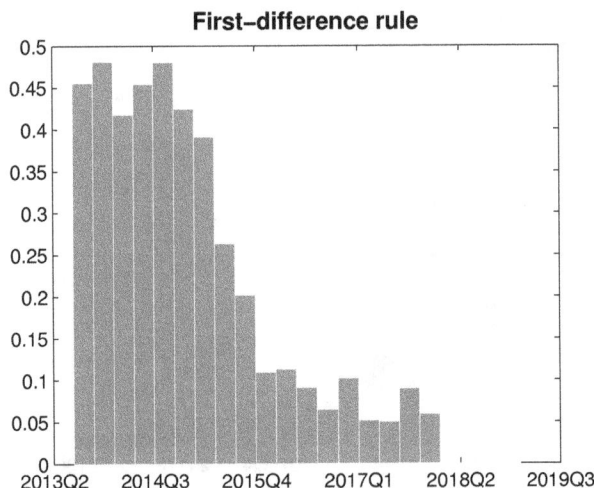

Figure 4
Optimal policies versus the inertial Taylor (1999) rule
(Baseline conditions)

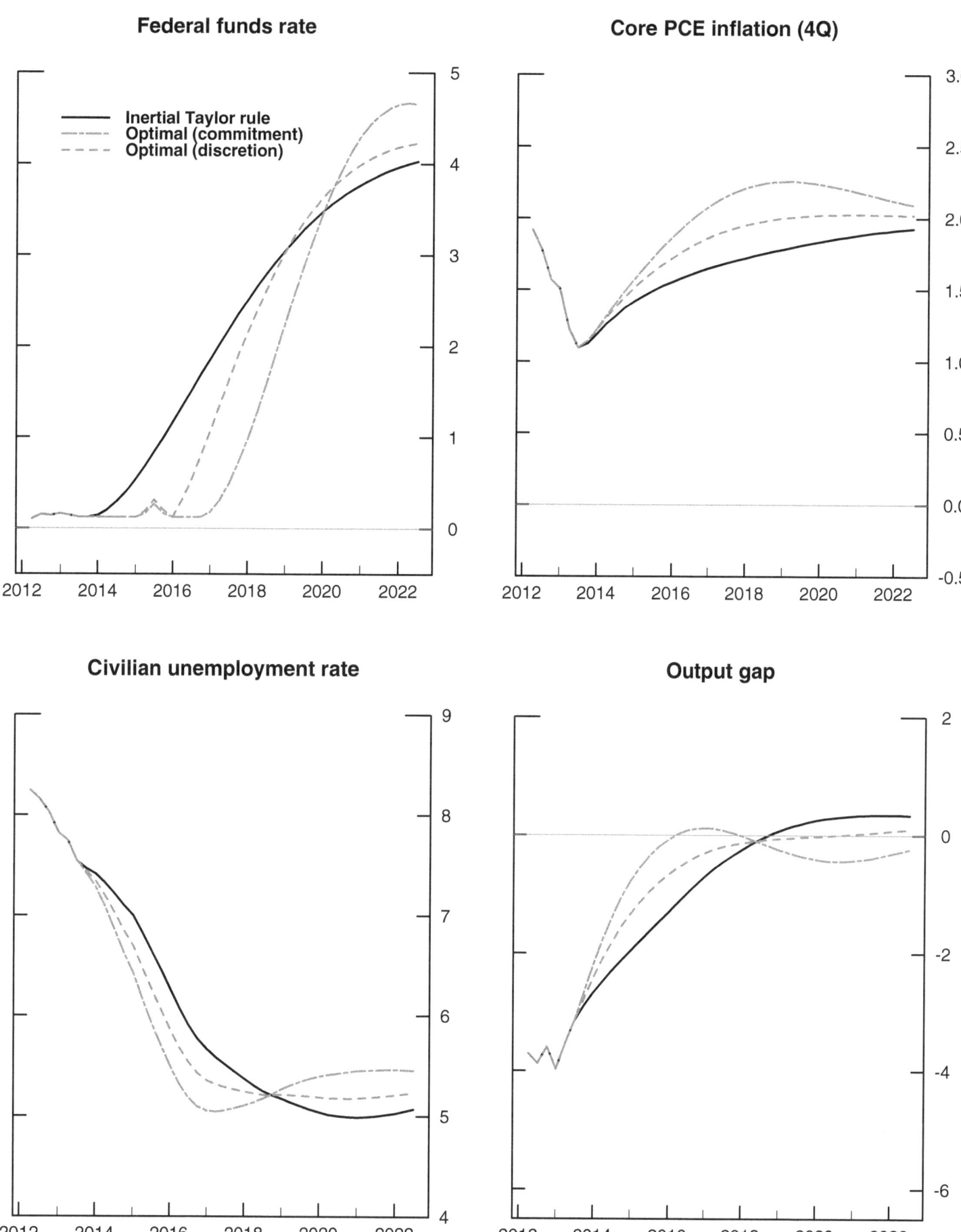

Federal funds rate

Inertial Taylor rule
Optimal (commitment)
Optimal (discretion)

Core PCE inflation (4Q)

Civilian unemployment rate

Output gap

Figure 5
Optimal and selected simple policy rules
(Baseline with larger absolute output gap)

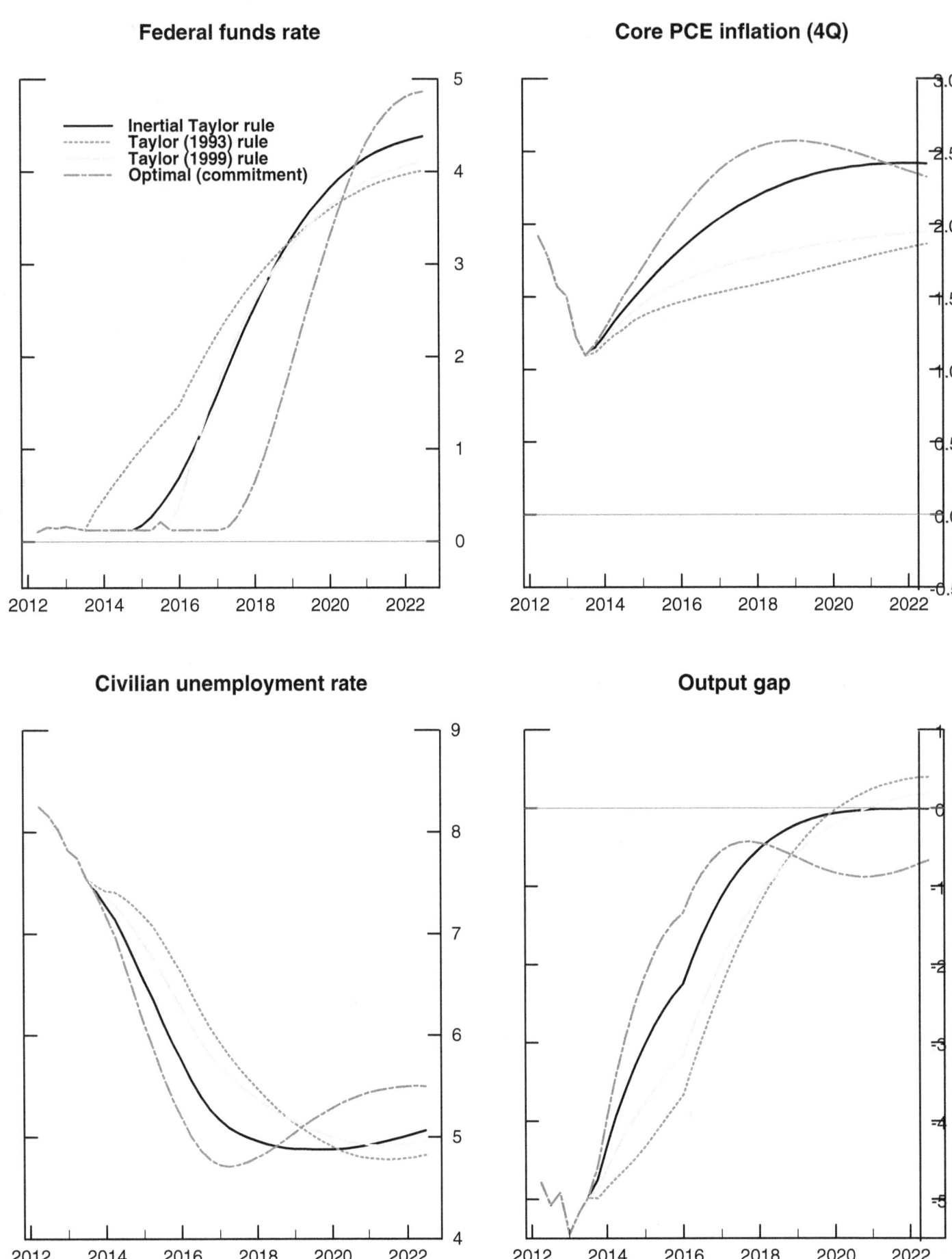

Federal funds rate

Inertial Taylor rule
Taylor (1993) rule
Taylor (1999) rule
Optimal (commitment)

Core PCE inflation (4Q)

Civilian unemployment rate

Output gap

Figure 6
Implications of alternative unemployment threshold values
(Inertial Taylor rule; Baseline conditions)

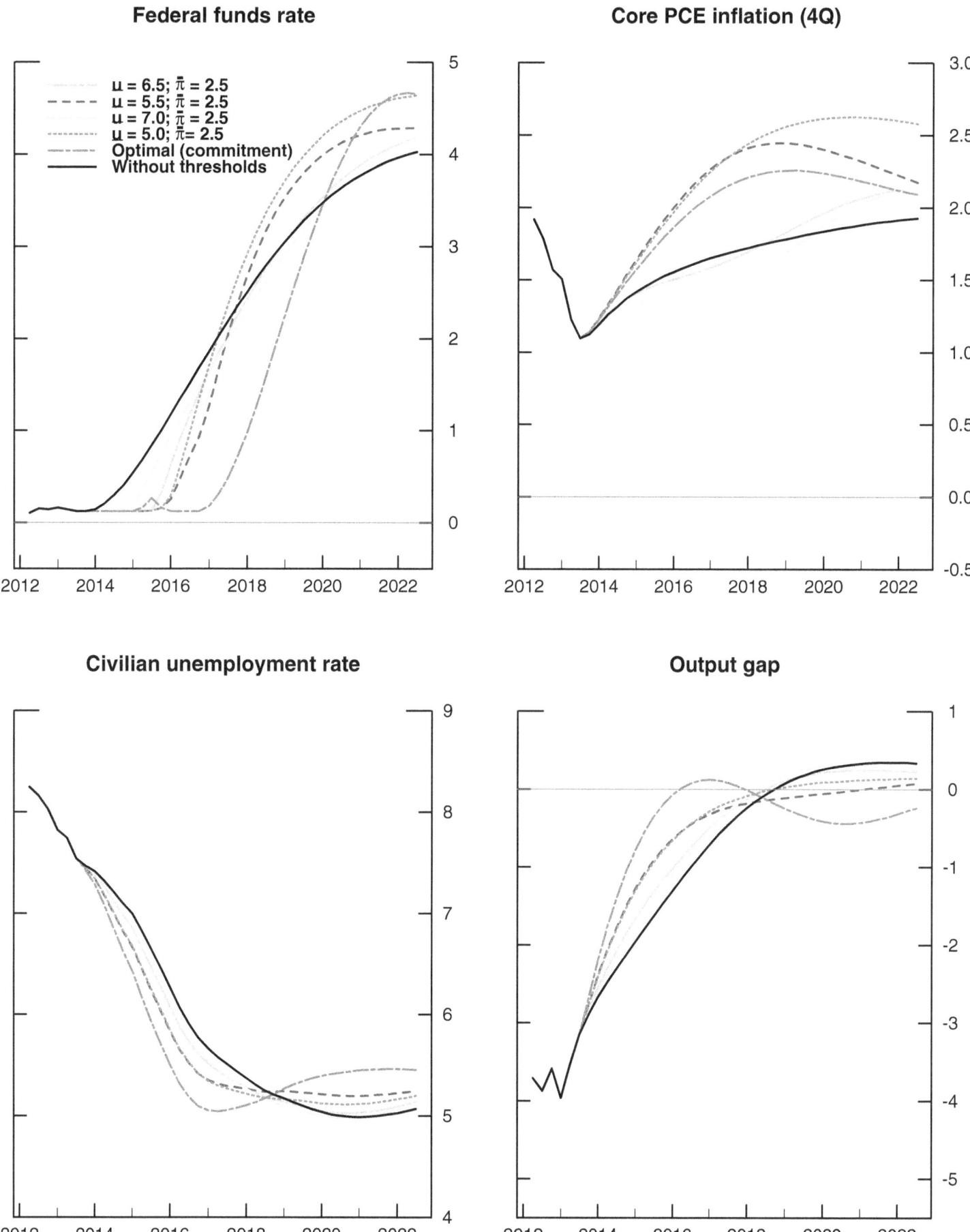

Federal funds rate

- u = 6.5; $\bar{\pi}$ = 2.5
- u = 5.5; $\bar{\pi}$ = 2.5
- u = 7.0; $\bar{\pi}$ = 2.5
- u = 5.0; $\bar{\pi}$ = 2.5
- Optimal (commitment)
- Without thresholds

Core PCE inflation (4Q)

Civilian unemployment rate

Output gap

Figure 7
Implications of alternative inflation threshold values
(Inertial Taylor rule; Baseline conditions)

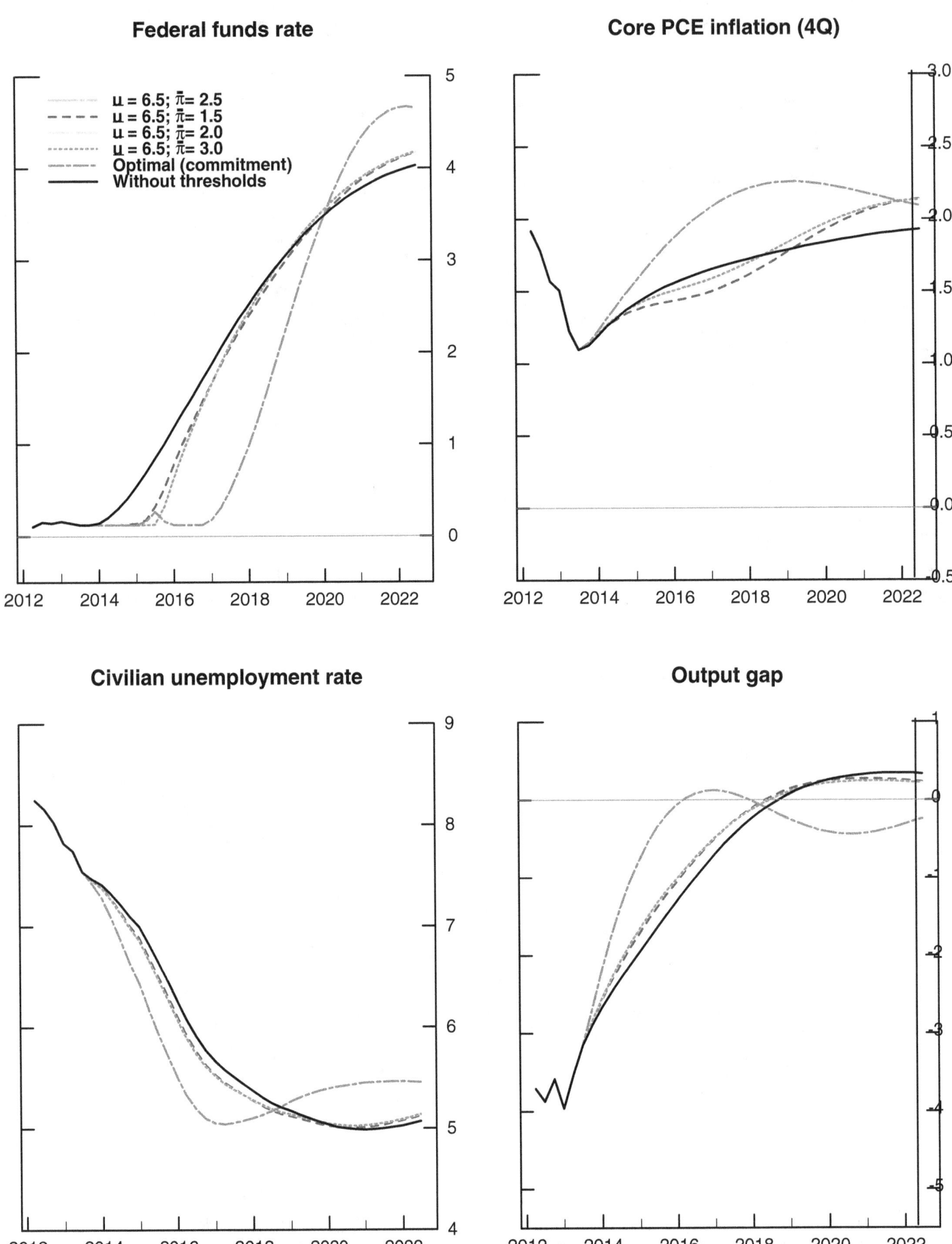

Federal funds rate

u = 6.5; π̄ = 2.5
u = 6.5; π̄ = 1.5
u = 6.5; π̄ = 2.0
u = 6.5; π̄ = 3.0
Optimal (commitment)
Without thresholds

Core PCE inflation (4Q)

Civilian unemployment rate

Output gap

Figure 8
Probability of liftoff from the effective lower bound by calendar date
(Stochastic simulations under inertial Taylor (1999) rule, with and without thresholds)

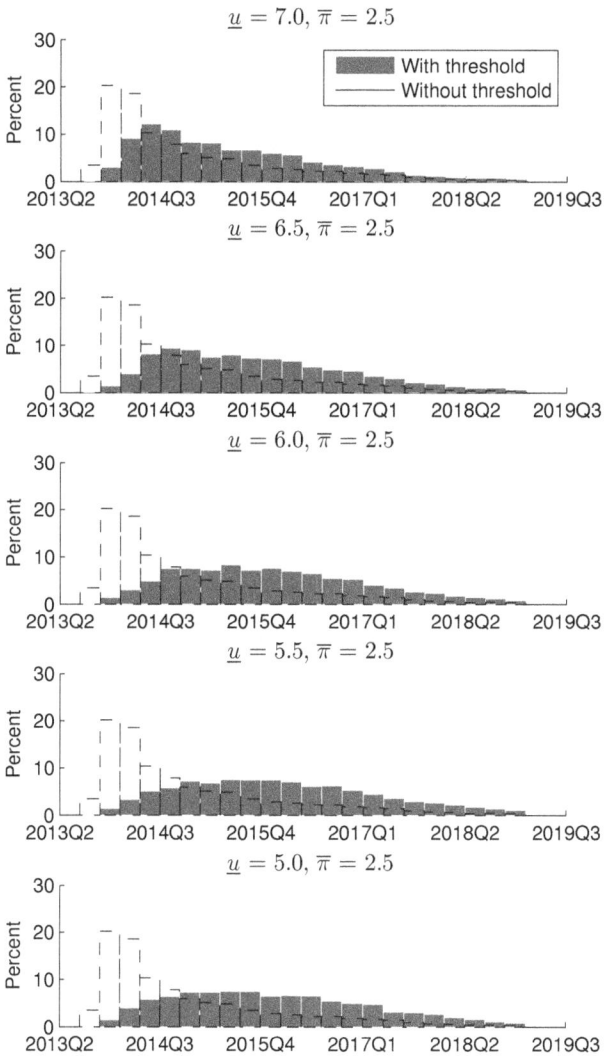
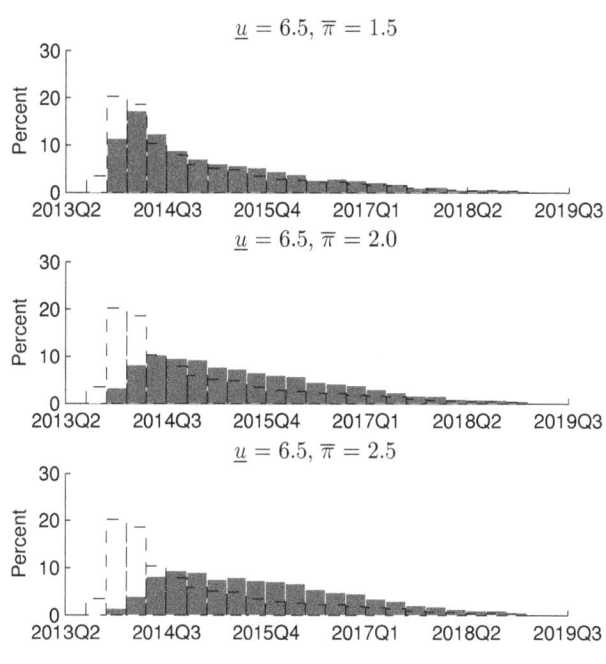

Figure 9
Probability of returning to the effective lower bound within four quarters of first liftoff
(Stochastic simulations under inertial Taylor (1999) rule, with and without thresholds)

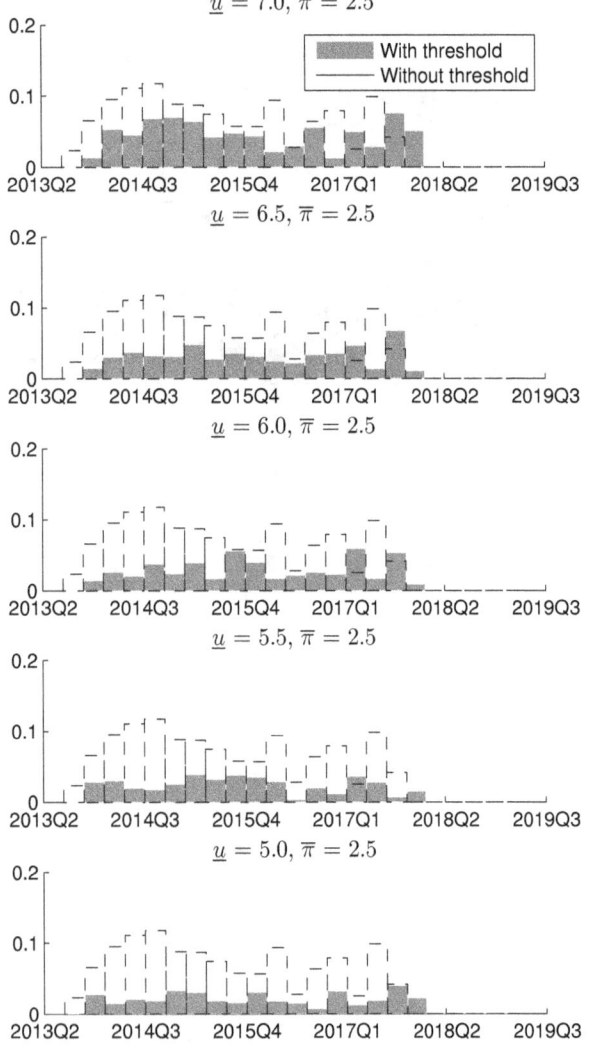

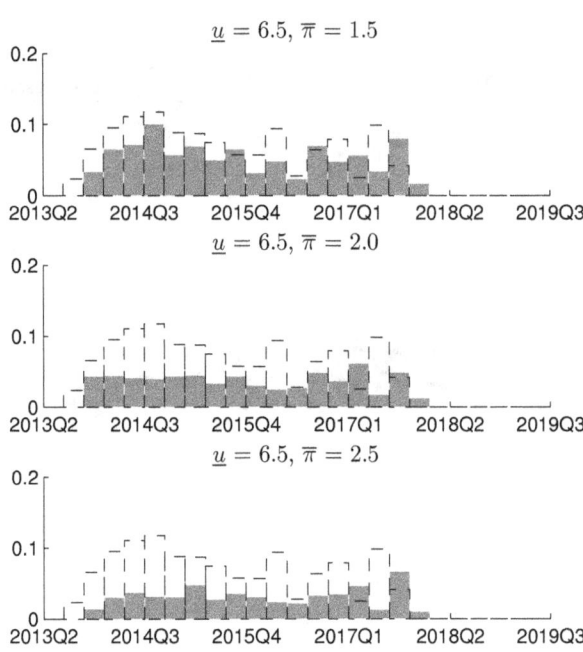

Figure 10
Increase in inflation target with and without policy credibility
(Inertial Taylor rule; Baseline conditions)

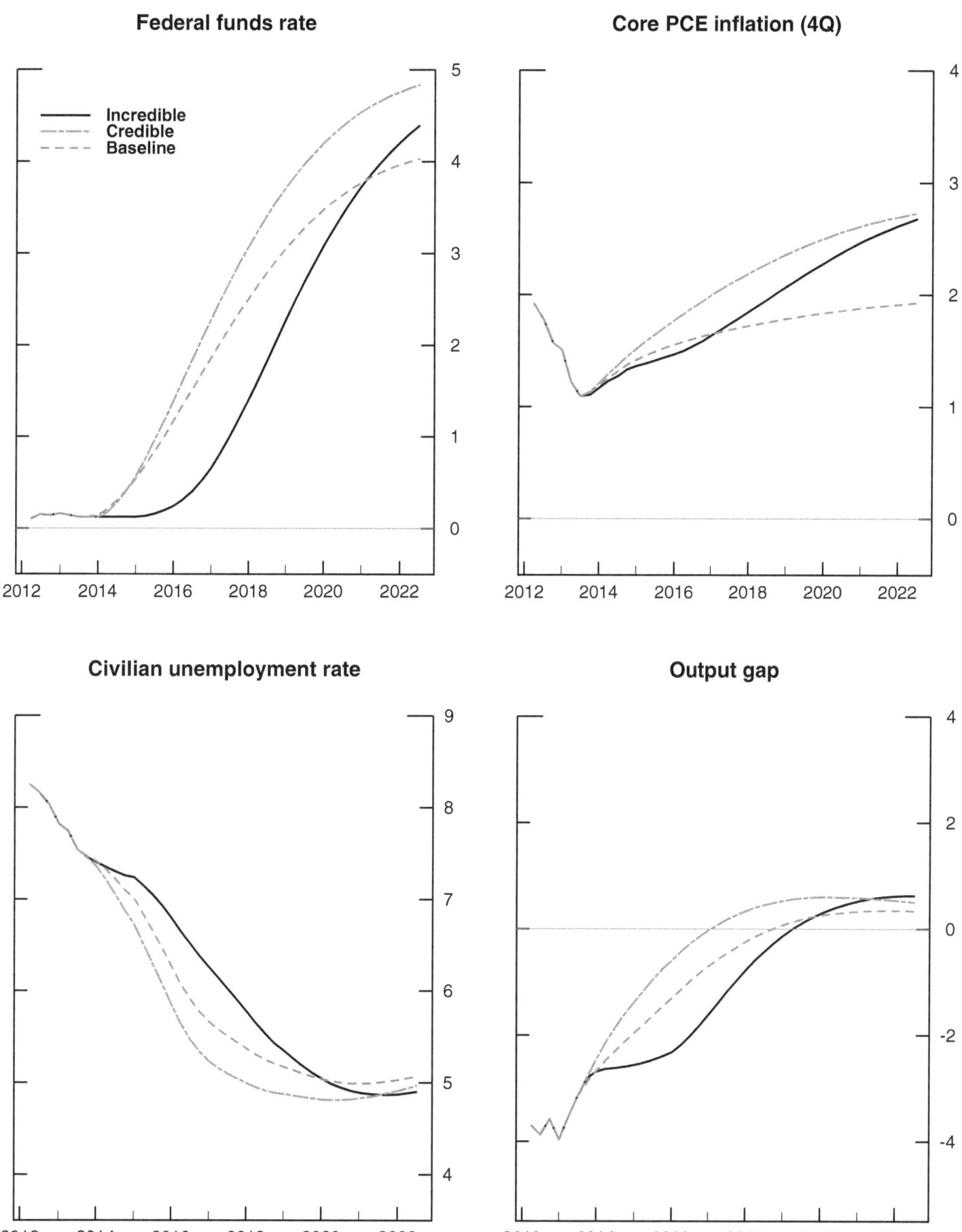

Federal funds rate

Incredible
Credible
Baseline

Core PCE inflation (4Q)

Civilian unemployment rate

Output gap

Figure 11
Nominal income level targeting
(Baseline conditions)

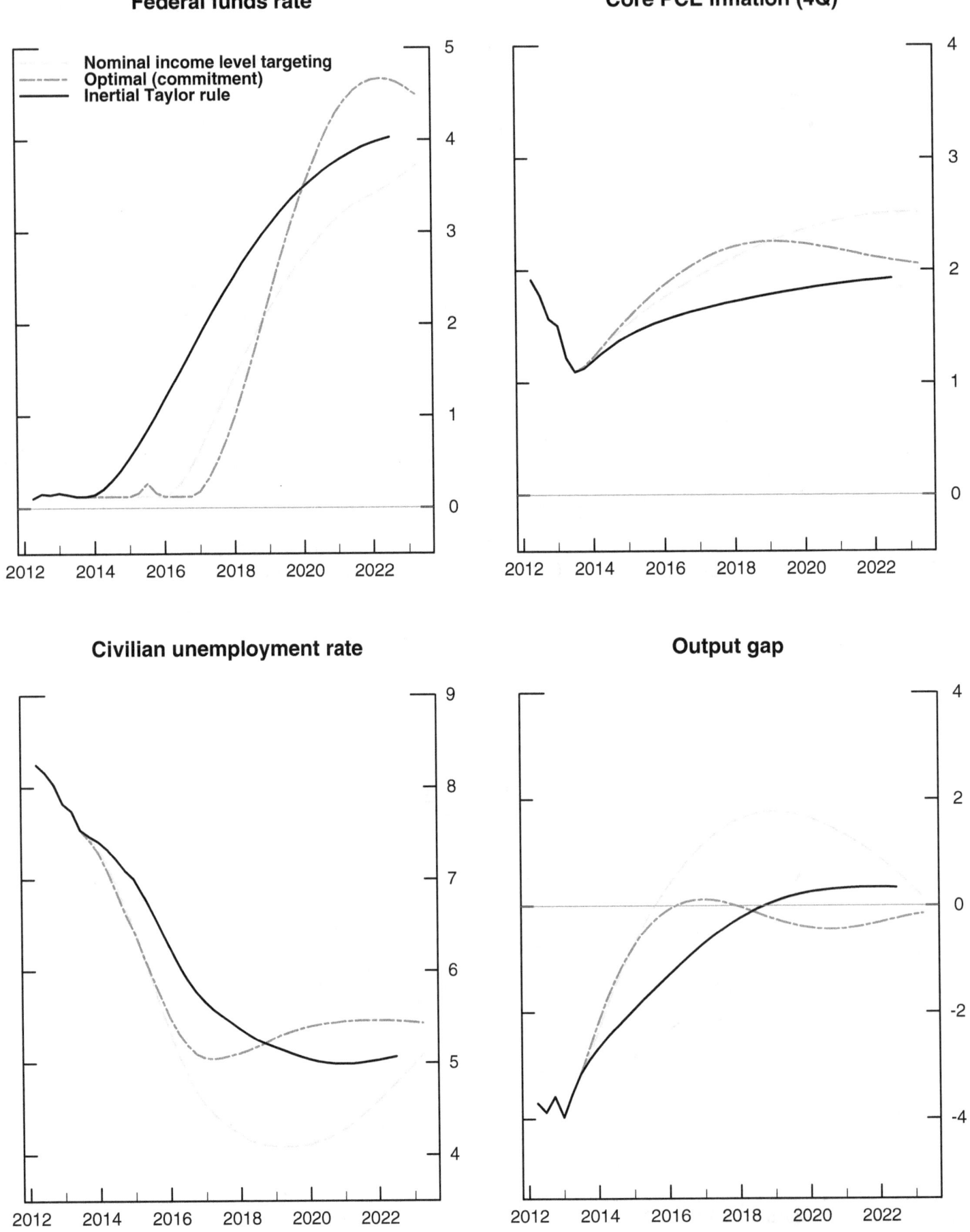

Federal funds rate

- Nominal income level targeting
- Optimal (commitment)
- Inertial Taylor rule

Core PCE inflation (4Q)

Civilian unemployment rate

Output gap

Figure 12
The level of nominal income by data vintage
(Selected dates and selected vintages)

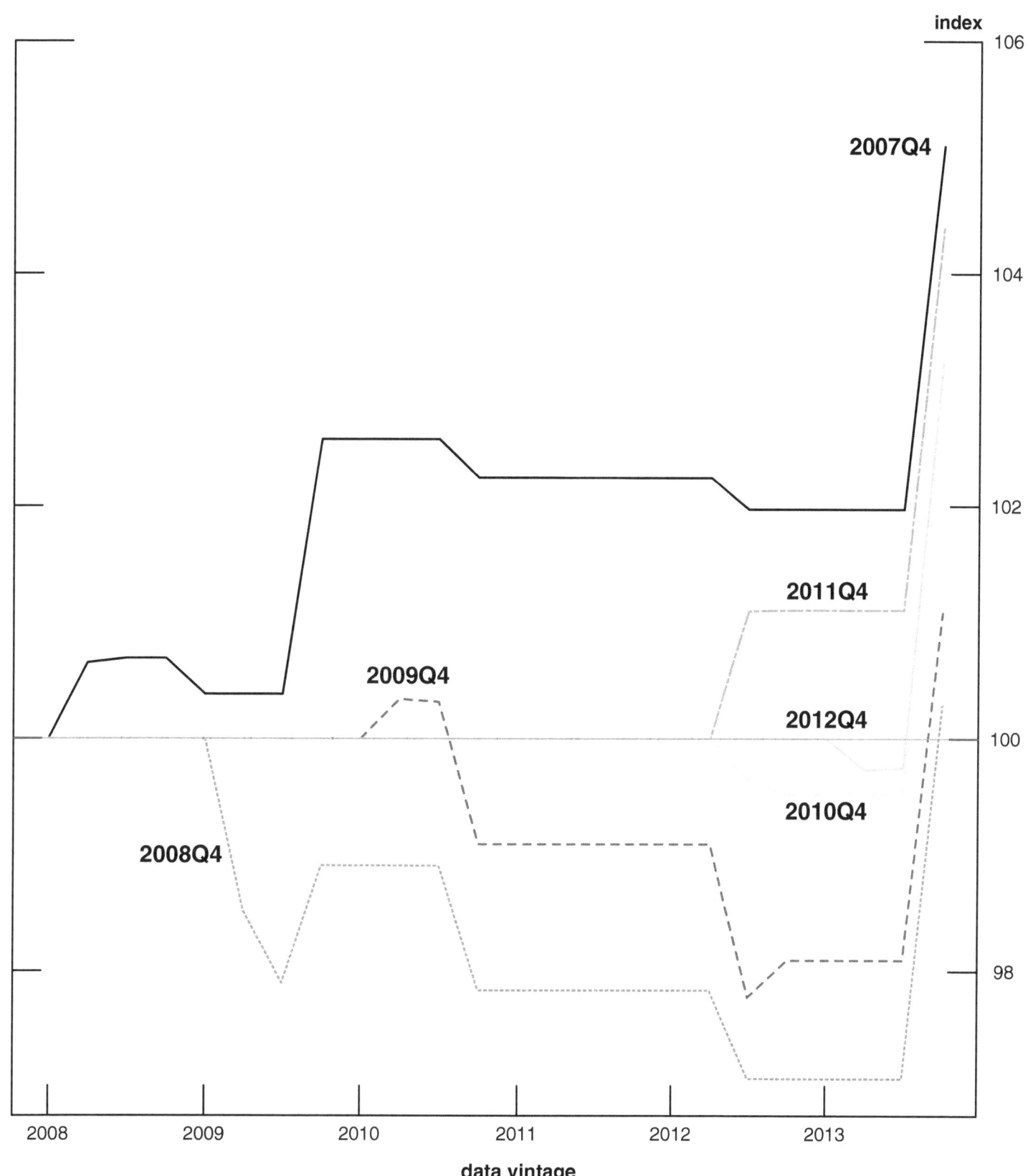

Figure 13
Effects of different initial nominal-income-level gaps
(Nominal income level targeting)

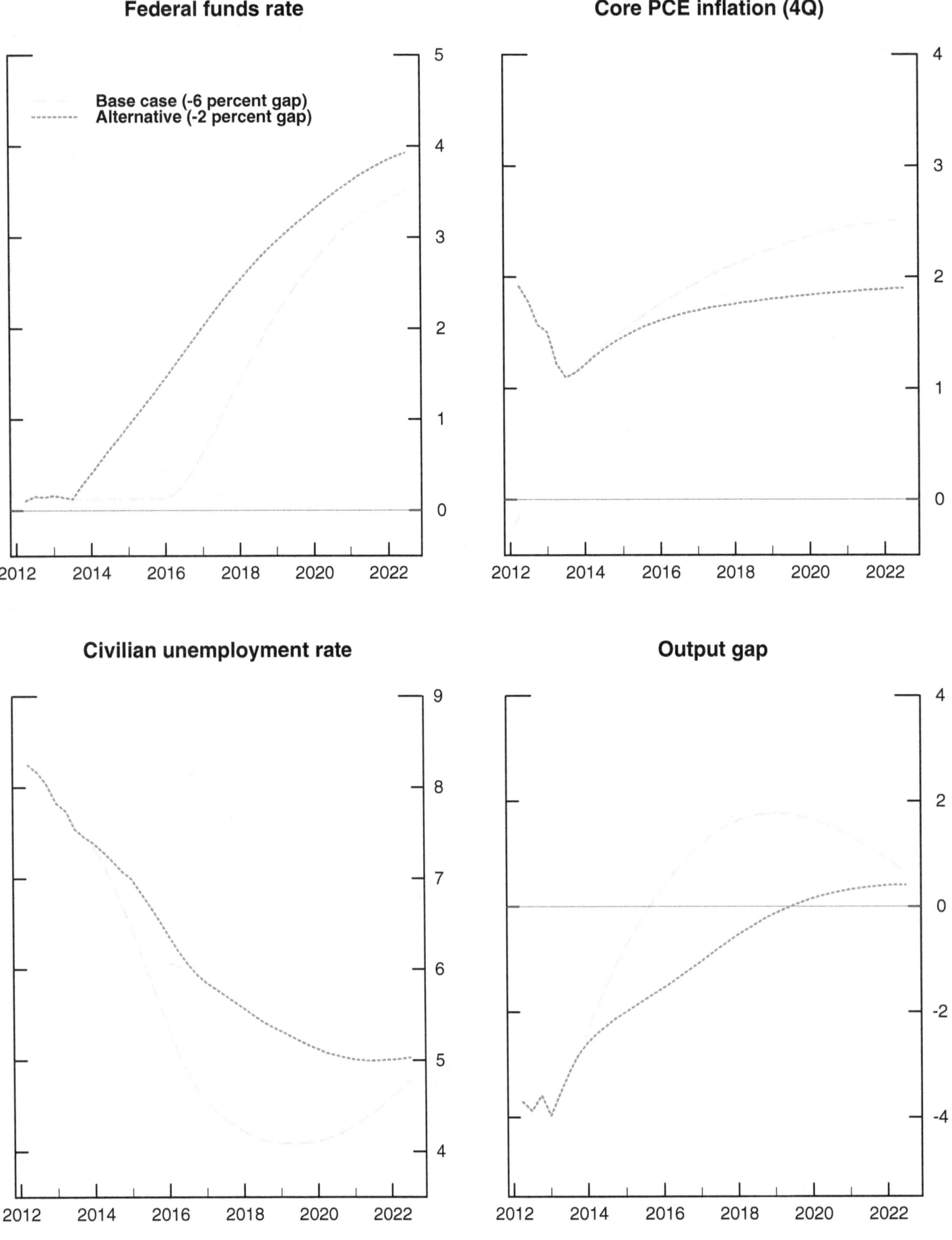

Federal funds rate

Base case (-6 percent gap)
Alternative (-2 percent gap)

Core PCE inflation (4Q)

Civilian unemployment rate

Output gap

Figure 14
Effects of expectations on policy outcomes
(Nominal income level targeting with and without complete information)

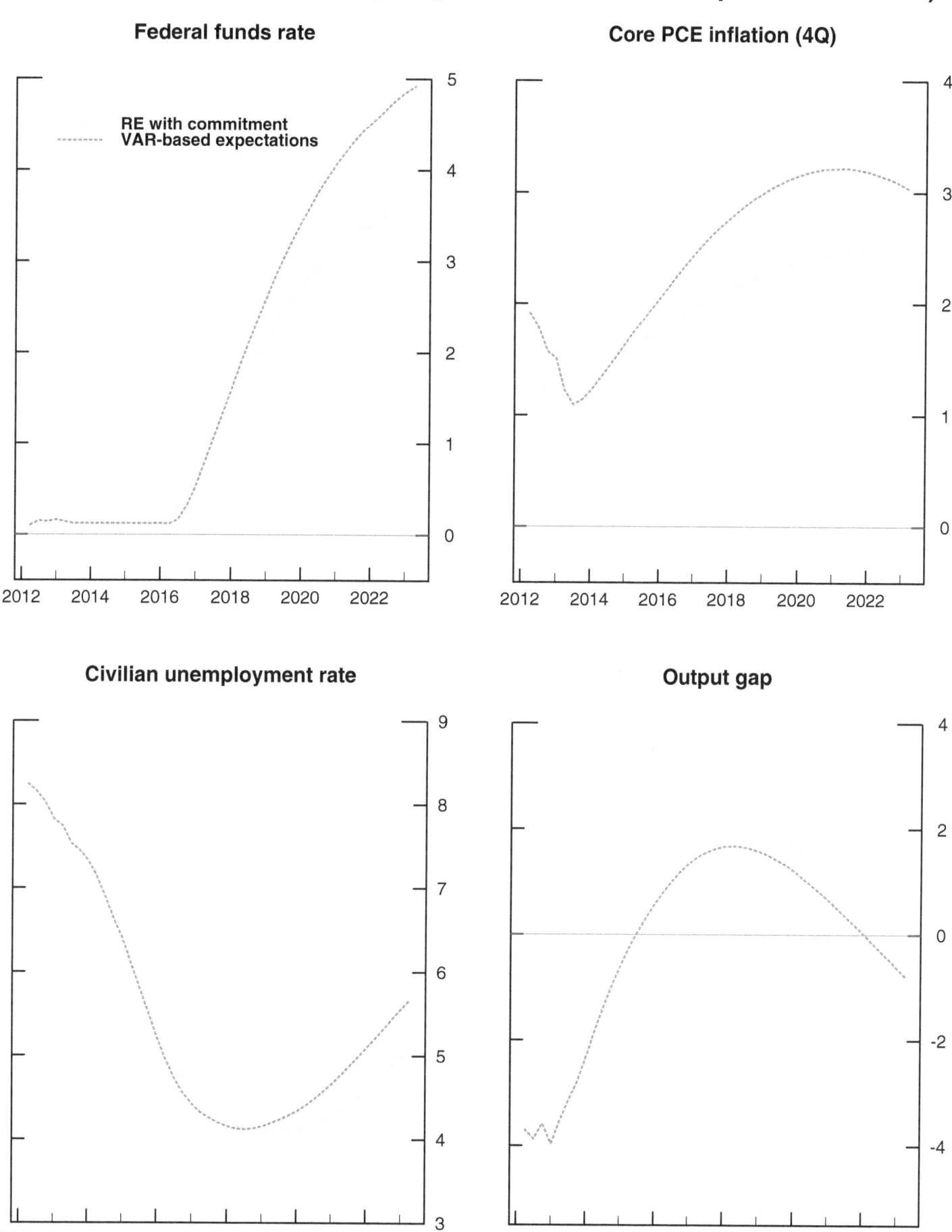

Federal funds rate

RE with commitment
VAR-based expectations

Core PCE inflation (4Q)

Civilian unemployment rate

Output gap